What to Expect When Your Wife Is Expanding

What to Expect When Your Wife Is Expanding

A Reassuring Month-by-Month Guide
for the Father-to-Be,
Whether He Wants Advice or Not

Thomas Hill, Registered Father, BA

**Andrews McMeel
Publishing, LLC**
Kansas City • Sydney • London

Andrews McMeel Publishing, LLC

an Andrews McMeel Universal company

1130 Walnut Street, Kansas City, Missouri 64106

www.andrewsmcmeel.com

12 13 14 15 16 RR4 10 9 8 7 6 5 4 3 2 1

ISBN: 978-1-4494-1846-5

Library of Congress Control Number: 2011945619

ATTENTION: SCHOOLS AND BUSINESSES

Andrews McMeel books are available at quantity discounts with bulk purchase for educational, business, or sales promotional use. For information, please e-mail the Andrews McMeel Publishing Special Sales Department: specialsales@amuniversal.com

To all my babies and former babies—
Deke, Frederica, Parker, Bixby, Walker, and Griffin
—but they all have to wait till they're grown-up to read it!

And to my inspiring and loving wife, Michelle.

Contents

Contents

Contents

Contents

Contents

Contents

PREFACE TO THE THIRD EDITION

How This Book Was Conceived ... Again

Let's be honest, when I first set out to write this book, four or five babies ago (more on that in a moment), my editor and I were thinking a quick parody pregnancy guide for men would offer plenty of material for comedy and might even be a little bit useful. Well, our spoof was embraced by readers as a welcome lighthearted take on this awesome experience. *Expanding* became a staple gift for expectant husbands, a surprising grassroots success that just keeps finding new audiences. Now, with this edition, it is thoroughly updated and, yes, expanded, with so much all-new material it's like being pregnant for eleven months!

First things first. Not unlike a husband to a pregnant wife, the book serves as an affable, funny, half-informed, well-meaning companion to the pregnancy books that do the real work. More than anything, we hope to offer expectant parents a good laugh or two. We also hope you come away with some genuine reassurance and maybe even some hard-won advice and wisdom, the balanced perspective that comes from real-world experience. That I've got. In singular devotion to my subject, I have had six children (over two marriages). My most recent child was born in 2011, as the result of a pregnancy coinciding neatly with the writing of this edition. Now that's doing research! I know, I know. Divorce, remarriage, six kids. It does seem like a lot of trouble to go through just to make sure you have a thoroughly accurate and up-to-date accounting of a father's experience. That's just the kind of author I am. Dedicated. I even managed to lift enough heavy babies to damage my wrist and thumb in a form of tendonitis that is (I swear) called new mom's syndrome. Apparently, it most often occurs in new mothers, whose ligaments have been loosened by pregnancy, then stressed by baby lifting. I prefer the more scientific and masculine name—De Quervain's tenosynovitis—although I'd really prefer not to have had it at all.

Now cynics may question my judgment when it comes to writing about relationships. Let me assure you that when it comes to relationships I have never had the slightest idea what I'm talking about. I don't know what women want or why they do the things they do. Like most men, I simply remain dedicated to finding out, one baffling request at a time. And I can tell you, as a general guide, that happily married is more fun than unhappily married.

When it comes to pregnancy and childbirth, there have been technical advances and further research over the last decade, so that now there are literally scores of new fears, anxieties, and dietary strictures to deal with. Luckily, "provoking anxiety" has gone totally out of fashion. Not so long ago, the core philosophy was that a new mother deserved to know every possible problem or outcome. Today, the experts agree that too much information breeds too much needless anxiety. So relax! When the time comes to worry about venous thrombosis or partial molar pregnancy, the doctors will tell you. We do recommend using a doctor.

Yes, pregnancy hasn't really changed much, nor have the eternal differences between men and women that are at the core of this book. Those differences are worth both celebration and laughter and, let it be said at the outset, well worth bridging. So in all seriousness (for just about the last time in these pages), congratulations on your impending fatherhood, and best wishes to your wife, as well. My only real advice is this: Take care of each other, and the baby will take care of itself. Not *literally*, but you get the point.

—Thomas Hill

Why This Book Was Conceived

It used to be so easy for us dads. The rabbit would die; only her doctor had to hear the monthly details. After all, it was all in the realm of "female trouble." Our responsibility was to take one frantic drive to the hospital, to spend a few hours pacing, and *voilà!* Progeny! Pass out the cigars. Those were the days when every newborn came with an undebatable last name.

Everything has changed. Good news for those rabbits, but not for the expectant father. And in case you're wondering, yes, not so many years ago, laboratory technicians really did have to knock off a bunny for every single pregnancy test that came out positive. (What sicko invented that?) But we were talking about today's father. He has a dozen new roles: birthing coach, dietician, masseur, interior decorator, butler, psychotherapist, tugboat to her barge, and others. Furthermore, he is expected to be well versed in all of pregnancy's medical details, options, and research, up to and including the current issue of the *American Journal of Obstetrics & Gynecology*, and should also be sensitive enough to know from across the room

when the baby is kicking. All this, and he doesn't even get a healthy glow. What *about* the father? What about *his* needs, *his* problems, *his* concerns?

What to Expect When Your Wife Is Expanding is the book we wished we could have turned to in our own moments of crisis, self-doubt, and, perhaps most of all, boredom. Everything you need to know about the next nine months is in the pages that follow, although of course you don't really "need" to know anything, except possibly that *psychoprophylaxis* is the scientific term for birth preparedness training and does *not* mean birth control through telekinesis. And now you know that.

Some may say it is only fair and natural that all books on the subject have focused on the female experience of pregnancy. Women are doing all the real work, right? Let's face it: You were necessary only for about 15 minutes last July. No matter how much you do as a pregnant pop, nobody will ever practice kung fu on *your* bladder from the inside. Nobody takes over *your* body and soul for nine months. (Ten months, actually; more on that later.) Isn't the woman doing all the real suffering? Isn't your wife the one who can't smoke one cigarette or have one glass of wine and is supposed to drink milk by the pailful and can't eat any foods she likes and is gaining tons of weight anyway (which is completely unfair) and doesn't even know how she will deal with the pain and is doing it all because *you* were so gung ho on starting a family?

And why do you need your own book? Why can't you just read all her pregnancy books and empathize? First of all, women just don't understand how hard it is to empathize. Ironic, ain't it? Second, why should she begrudge you one measly, modestly priced book? Finally, her books are all really long and don't have very many jokes in them.

Yes. Yes. Yes. The pregnant woman is the one who really deserves all the attention. But you'll be hearing all that from her. You've got a pregnant mate, but now you've got a book all your own. This is the other side of the story. We'll never call you a thoughtless slug. We know that facing all the new responsibilities, burdens, and duties of being a father, you need guidance, information, moral support. We know it's hard to be an expectant father even when she doesn't. Remember, you're pregnant, too! (Just be very selective about how often you tell her that.)

A Note on Pronouns

It is traditional in books about pregnancy and child care for the authors to attempt to justify the use of the masculine pronoun when referring to a generic baby. Some rationalize that it's just less confusing when "she" refers to the mother and "he" refers to the baby. (Which leaves us fathers out entirely, as usual.) Others find the "he or she" construction awkward. We are not so quick to bow to exigency and compromise.

Though it may take some getting used to, we have chosen to use an ampersand, circumflex, and pound sign (&^#) to indicate the nominative he or she and a possessive asterisk (*'s) in place of the possessive his or her. Our only concession to gender stereotyping is that in almost all cases we will assume *'s pregnant mother is a she.

But we have now changed our minds. (By the way, throughout the text I will refer to myself as "we," just because it seems more authoritative.) The solution in the paragraph above is obviously unwieldy. Perhaps we could just assume that you're having twins, one boy and one girl? When your babies are born, they will be . . . no, too anxiety provoking! Instead, we will attempt to avoid the issue completely by writing around as many pronouns as possible. Or we could call a baby "the baby," and use the grammatically incorrect "their" when we really should say "his or her":

for example, "When you first see Baby, you will want to nibble on their cute little toes." What do you want? Good grammar or gender neutrality? Furthermore, we may just slide into using "him or her" without even knowing it. Why are you reading this note anyway? Get to the text! You're having a baby, man, step to it!

A Note to the Mother-To-Be

We couldn't be more pleased that you are being supportive of your husband and reading *What to Expect When Your Wife Is Expanding.* Or perhaps you're reading it because your husband was hiding it in his sock drawer. Perhaps you bought it for him and want to make sure we're not out of line. Perhaps you've read every other pregnancy book and Web site you could find and are desperate. In any case, we're happy to have you here. Naturally, most of our comments are geared to a father's experience, but you shouldn't feel left out. Understanding what your husband is going through is the most important thing you can do. And don't forget that pregnancy can be just as challenging, rewarding, and involving for a woman as it is for a man.

By the way, perhaps we should be more open-minded, and we have no intention of getting embroiled in any Red State/Blue State debate about family values, but we feel strongly that a man shouldn't get pregnant on his own. Call us old-fashioned.

CHAPTER ONE

What to Expect When ... "You're What?"

"You're What?"

Does life begin as "a gleam in father's eye"?

This playful idiom is thoroughly outdated. Gleams are a nice start, but today pregnancy is more likely to be planned, discussed, even scheduled. Couples consider their careers, their finances, their health, their age, the results of their genetic counseling, the feng shui of their apartment, and the latest forecast for mortgage rates. Having a baby is complicated, expensive, painful, and messy, yet people keep doing it. Scientists and sociologists point to an increasingly convincing body of research that indicates this is largely a result of babies being so darn cute.

So, a gleam in father's eye? Quite the opposite, old boy. In fact, pregnancy may still begin with a gleam, but today that gleam is probably in *her* eye, and she's not thinking about you, gorgeous. There comes a time in life when you're just the means to a seven-pound, six-ounce end.

There is, naturally, the possibility of simultaneous eye gleaming (and we all know how much fun that can be). This can mean either a pair of equally baby-crazy parents or a pair of very surprised parents who weren't expecting to be expecting. Those who planned ahead are statistically more likely to invest in a wider variety of nursery wallpaper borders and baby books, but otherwise the differences are minimal. Once you start, you are all on the same path. Just because you're surprised doesn't mean you're not ready. Fate says you are, and the countdown to a new life—for you and the baby—started a month and a half ago. Not a morning person? Well, you will be soon enough.

Finally, there is the least common situation when the gleam actually *is* in the father's eye. When *you* really want to have kids and your wife has lingering doubts about stalling her career, sacrificing her body, and learning to love whatever animated characters or singing combos Nick Junior and Disney Preschool are hawking lately, well that is *trouble* mister. Danger, danger, danger! Sure, you might talk her into it, but as the wait goes on, and the weight goes on—she'll know *exactly* whom to blame. If you're eager to get started having babies, be very careful to make it seem like it was at least partly her idea. You might even want to get her to sign something.

No matter whose fault, we mean *idea*, it is, so many joys and experiences lie ahead. Before you ever become a father, you're going to be "pregnant." You'll try to record the amplified heartbeat in the fourth month. (It makes an odd but compelling ringtone!) You'll be parrying "Who's the father?" wisecracks from the boys. You'll nod knowingly, pretending you see it, while a doctor points at a piece of abstract art and claims it is a sonogram image of Baby's head, spine, or "small parts." And then you'll have that same ultrasound picture as a screen saver.

You'll go along with your wife when she puts your hand on her tummy and says, "There, you *had* to feel that one." You'll debate the issue of paternity leave. Can you take it? And if you take it, can you take it? How long can anyone take it? You'll organize the Date-Weight-Sex Trifecta betting pools at the office for fun and profit, and, if you're like the average man, you'll repaint the nursery 2.7 times before she likes the color despite the fact that she shouldn't be anywhere near those fumes.

You'll wonder about life with Baby. Will you ever see your single friends again? And how will you explain that, yes, you do need to go home even though, yes, your wife is capable of watching the baby alone? How can you man up while wearing a baby in a sling? With a burp cloth draped over one shoulder? How will you deal with problems of rivalry? No, not what happens with siblings, but what will happen when you and the baby vie for your wife's attention? Have you properly bonded with your baby? Why do they always pee the moment the diaper comes off? Exactly how far does vomiting have to travel to be defined as "projectile?"

But let's face it. If you've read this far, you're probably already a pregnant dad, or possibly just a member of the author's family (Hi, Mom! Hi, Dad!), but in either case, you're committed. You're going to be pregnant for a while, so you might as well go ahead and read this whole book while it might still seem funny. You know, when it is all happening to other people.

What It's Darn Important to Know about Prepregnancy Tests

Judging whether a woman is going to have a baby is a relatively simple matter of physiology. A home test or visit to a doctor can answer your question quickly and definitively. Judging whether a woman is in a state of prepregnancy is a much more subtle matter. However, it is vitally important for you to know whether she is prepregnant. If such a condition exists, the sooner you know, the better. Once you know, you can institute either proactive or evasive action.

The simplest test for determining prepregnancy is to listen to your wife. If you pay attention (for a change), you'll be able to discern a notable increase in suggestive comments: "Don't you think Zoë is a pretty name?" "Did you know there's a nice little nursery school just over on Elm Street?" or "My sister wants to know if we want Willy's crib now that he's out of it." These are clues. Are you picking up on them? If not, try reading this paragraph again. Think. What is this woman trying to tell you? Got it? There you go.

If listening to your wife is a challenge, if you had to read that last paragraph more than twice, or if you simply never know what she is getting at, it may be worth investing in one of the many books on the market aimed at improving male–female communication. A few recommended titles: Mary Cornwall, *What Women Don't Tell Men but Expect Them to Know* (Prentice-Schuster, 2007); E. P. Dunham, *Dictionary of the Female Language*, 15th edition (Oxford Reference Books, 2011); Robin Filmoore, *I Am Listening; You're Not Saying Anything!* (Freedentia College Press, 2008).

If you don't have time to read up on communication, or even to watch *The View* on a regular basis, you still have the list below to help you make this important determination.

The early warning signs of prepregnancy:

POSSIBLE
- Suggests "sex"
- Switches to organic vegetables and buys a water filter for the sink
- Expresses new concern for your diet; buys you omega-3 supplements
- Buys a DVD of *Mary Poppins*—not to watch, just to have
- Suggests your home office would make a nice bedroom
- Increasing use of cute nicknames: calls you "Li'l Bear," the cat "Meowzi," her toothbrush "the brusherwusher"
- Shows extreme, even giddy interest in other people's babies
- Renewed interest in real estate

PROBABLE
- Changes the home page on your browser to BabyCenter.com
- Responds to your sexual advances by taking her temperature
- Continues to use cute pet names and now speaks in extended periods of baby talk: "Oh! 'itty Snuggums made-all gone with his beer."
- Keeps forgetting birth control
- Shows increased interest in the whole "stability" concept: pension plans, mortgages, dogs, neighborhood beautification projects
- Starts knitting baby booties, or knitting anything pastel
- Stops drinking
- Stops smoking
- Stops swearing, to set a good example

DEFINITE

- Begins calling you "Daddy"
- Wants to make love twice a day for the three days around Thursday the twentieth
- Says, "I want to have a baby."
- Throws away birth control
- Paints and furnishes the nursery
- Schedules a "conceptionmoon vacation"—like a honeymoon, but with a purpose
- Says, "I said, I want to have a baby."

What You Should Have Known About Home Pregnancy Tests *Before* You Bought This Book

Rapid Response, FirstAlert, EPT Warning System. Not only is it difficult to choose from among the many home pregnancy testing kits that are available, but all three of these are actually home smoke alarms—and you don't want to come home with the wrong thing entirely. If you do, of course, you can cover by saying that your plans to start a family have made you more safety conscious, but you still won't know whether the bun is in the figurative oven. All you'll know is if there are buns burning in your literal oven. By the way, do not use the phrase "bun in the oven" at all until you have ascertained that your wife does not have a virulent reaction to it. Some do. "Bump" is another one.

The pharmaceutical companies have invested millions of dollars in the development of accurate, dependable, and easy-to-use home pregnancy tests. When these products first appeared on the over-the-counter market years ago, they were still untrustworthy, giving many false positives, false negatives, and occasional readings of "a negative times a negative is a positive," which is mathematically sound but leaves the pregnancy situation foggy. The early tests were approximately 75 percent as accurate as a good solid hunch.

Fabulous scientific breakthroughs, too complex for us to actually research, have made these at-home tests remarkably accurate. Today, they are considered almost as reliable as a doctor's blood test, and who cares whether your doctor is pregnant anyway? Let her buy her own test.

Accuracy was achieved (at great expense, which you've probably noticed has been passed on to you, the consumer), but ease of use came more slowly. The early systems involved mixing chemicals, warming solutions, waiting for hours—and thus left much room for error. Worse yet, no one could decide on the appropriate indicator. Should a little strip turn pink? Should a little ball turn blue? Should a little cartoon stork appear? The choice of visual indicator greatly depends on whether you are marketing these tests to hopeful young couples or to freaked-out high school seniors. For now, they seem to have settled on a relatively neutral design aesthetic: plus signs, or simple bars of color.

But look for niche marketing soon. The division is too vast to straddle. Perhaps "Wild Thing" for the teen market, with the slogan "When ya gotta know right now, for sure." For the older crowd, something more high-toned: perhaps "Genesis" with the slogan "Let There Be Light." We certainly hope that both will still boast, as current products have: "Just hold it in your urine stream!" Now that's an appealing line of advertising copy.

WHAT YOU MAY BE CONCERNED ABOUT

The Job of Sex

Q. *"We're not pregnant yet, and yes, we know how it's done; but ever since we started trying to get pregnant, sex just isn't what it used to be. And we're still not pregnant."*

A. Science has shown compelling evidence that sex is linked to pregnancy. So don't give up on this basic approach. Until they start marketing in vitro fertilization kits over the counter, it appears that if you're going to have a baby, you pretty much have to do "it." This process can be complicated, tiring, and sometimes disorienting, but don't forget that it can also be a loving and enjoyable one. Even fun, once you get the hang of it.

It may be hard to conceive, but for many couples, making the switch from recreational sex to procreational sex can be nerve-racking. Taking vitamin supplements, cutting down on caffeine and alcohol, checking the calendar, and taking her temperature are not traditionally thought of as foreplay. Subconsciously, you may still have doubts about whether you are ready for fatherhood.

The exact reasons are unclear, but more and more research is pointing to stress as a cause of fertility issues. It makes sense. Nature is saying that a woman already in stress is probably not a good candidate to be saddled with a hungry, wailing little eight-pound stress maker. As we warned you earlier, there are now things called "conceptionmoons"—a vacation with the specific purpose of setting stress aside and letting nature take its course. Yes, sir, nothing like a week away with no plans, no pressure, and no goal except to conceive a baby. That'll relax any guy. Can't you almost feel your sperm count dropping?

Another factor on the plus side is that you are now working with the terrific advantage of not using birth control. (If you are still using birth control, that could be your problem right there.) In general, just try to forget about the ends and concentrate on the means. Think positive, and muddle your way through it—after all, once you have a baby, you'll hardly ever have sex at all!

Goo Goo Google

Q. *"Do I really have to read a whole book about pregancy? Before my brother-in-law gave me this book, I was just planning on doing a quick Internet search whenever issues came up."*

A. Fine, don't read the book; but before you go, take one last piece of advice. The Internet is a great place to get late-breaking injury reports on football players, watch YouTube videos of complete strangers embarrassing themselves, or reacquire all the Dark Knight comics your mother sold at a tag sale the week you went to college. However, it can be a dangerous place to get information about becoming a father.

Surfing the Internet is not really like surfing at all, but more like being dragged (and clicked) out to sea by three different undertows. You will quickly find yourself swept away, floating untethered, drowning in a watery morass from which no amount of "back" clicking can rescue you. Distractions lurk everywhere, from up-to-the-minute sports scores to wonderful opportunities in real estate to the latest news on Paris Hilton's "career."

Go ahead, Google "father" or "becoming a father." Type carefully: (Did you mean Fathead?) Or wait until some medical question comes up. You'll soon find that instead of a few simple, reassuring answers, you'll have access to articles from medical research journals complete with footnotes and laboratory methodology. Want information on babies? Whose? Angelina Jolie's? Celebrity baby photos are an Internet obsession that will do you little good. Want to see the incredible-but-true Web site about the world's first pregnant man? It was still out there last time we looked, drawing in the gullible with one of the most elaborate hoax sites ever created.

What can you search for? We don't have to tell you that Googling "Sex During Pregnancy" is not going to lead you to the pragmatic health advice you are no doubt seeking. When it comes to pregnancy in general, the various search algorithm methods are about as reliable as the "rhythm method." (Look it up on Wikipedia if you don't get that joke.) There are plenty of other wrong suggestions and strange links to be stumbled upon. Here are just a few:

1. Looking for "paternity leave advice," I found lots of "fight for your paternity rights" custody lawyers.

2. Looking for "cloth or disposable," I found biodegradable fabrics available in bulk for eco-designers.

3. Looking for "bonding with Baby," I found lots of bail-bond companies willing to spring before you spend even one night in jail.

4. Looking for "paternity leave," I entered a typo and found the Facebook page for some poor soul in Norway named Paatern Tylevenson.

5. Looking for "how will the dog react?" I found "Who Let the Dogs Out? Ring tone available now!"

6. Looking for "this week's hot waiver wire wide receivers," I found them. Well, there's always a little time to tweak that fantasy roster!

7. Looking for "lactation consultants, local," I found "chat live with hot lactating mamas." Not to get too judgmental, but eew. Seriously. By comparison, that makes foot fetishists seem positively charming.

8. Still looking for "taking paternity leave advice," I found old episode listings for the *Jerry Springer* show.

Now, there are indeed some worthwhile sites and resources. WhatToExpect.com, naturally. BabyCenter.com is well decorated with sponsor links—but the core site has everything you need, including a way to register your due date and get weekly e-mails that will, at the very least, remind you to ask your wife how she is feeling. For those of you who just got married, making the switch from TheKnot.com to TheNest.com will

be a comforting transition. For prospective fathers seeking a particularly macho approach—try *Dads Adventure*, a vaguely military approach to diaper changing and baby wrangling.

All in all, let me assure you that your brother-in-law's purchase was a sound investment and well worth reading. This book is not only portable and easy on the eyes but also tangible proof that you truly care about your wife's experience, the pregnancy, and every little symptom and possibility. That is gold, my friend.

Q. Emotional Maturity
"Am I ready for this?"

A. Sure you are. Well, all right, maybe you're not, but your wife is, and she can help you out with the fine points of emotional maturity. Anyway, by the time you're reading this book, the question is very likely moot. So why did you even ask?

If you are still having doubts, don't worry. Maturity isn't as complicated as psychotherapists would like you to believe. Becoming a mature, responsible, thoughtful, supportive, loving, giving, self-controlled, and self-aware person is really just a matter of behavior modification. Start with the following list, find the immature behavior that you currently practice, and simply force yourself to choose the modified alternative. As

Immature Behavior vs. Modified Maturity

Openly and proudly collecting baseball cards	Scouting eBay in order to accurately assess the current market value of your collection
Buying new clothes to look good for chicks	Buying new clothes to look good for your superiors at work
Needing time alone to chill	Needing time alone to work things out
Buying a car that has great acceleration and sleek lines	Buying the same car because it has antilock brakes, extra room in the back, latch seat restraints, and a good write-up in *Consumer Reports*
Never making the bed because you're just going to get back into it again	Making the bed because it's a relatively easy way to make her happy
Drinking too much when out with friends	Drinking too much in the privacy of your own home
One-ringing your college roommate to let him know his team is getting thumped	One-ringing your college roommate to make sure your cell reception is working
Setting up a computer program to keep track of your fantasy football team	Setting up a computer program to keep track of your family finances
Playing the stereo too loudly	Telling the neighbors they're playing their stereo too loudly
Watching the game	Checking the score
Collecting beer cans	Recycling beer cans
Being amused at exploits of eccentric or hard-partying friends from college	Being concerned about eccentric or hard-partying friends from college

you'll see, in some cases you don't even have to modify your behavior, just your explanation. After some initial backsliding, you'll find yourself behaving like a mature adult—as long as you stick to the chart. And in time, you may begin acting like a grown-up on a regular basis simply out of habit. Before you know it, you'll even feel ready to be a daddy. Then you'll have the baby, stop getting enough sleep, and completely regress, but you can fall off that bridge when you come to it. In the meantime, get to work.

A Bundle of Joy

Q. *"How much does having a baby cost?"*

A. If you have to ask, you're grasping at straws. Cost is no reason not to have a baby. A baby can be absolutely free. With home birth, breastfeeding, and the inevitable deluge of hand-me-downs, the setup costs can be minimal. Try gathering nuts and berries, and by the time your child is six he will be pulling his own weight. However, the question remains: Given a more typical contemporary lifestyle, can you afford a baby? The following chart will allow you to plan and budget, just as long as your baby agrees to grow naturally straight teeth.

ITEM	COST	WHAT ELSE YOU COULD DO WITH THE MONEY	COST-SAVING TIP
Labor and delivery	$6,000–$8,000	Buy a decent used car.	Consider home birth.
Gifts, dining out, flowers to get wife through pregnancy	$3,200	Take an excellent domestic vacation.	Compose poems and love letters, instead.
Pregnancy guidebooks; baby-name books; Spock in hardcover	$125	Salute Sam Raimi by buying DVDs of all the *Evil Dead* movies and the first two *Spider-Mans*.	Borrow from ex-pregnant friends.

ITEM	COST	WHAT ELSE YOU COULD DO WITH THE MONEY	COST-SAVING TIP
Clothing (per year)	$950	Buy complete collectible reprints of *Batman* daily comic strips from the 1940s. Hey, you spend your $950 the way you want; that's what I want.	Wear hand-me-downs.
Allowance ages 0–8	$3,000	Spend a seriously wild weekend in Vegas.	Practice tough love.
Haircuts, ages 0–18	$1,150	Buy a decent plasma flat-screen HDTV.	Cut hair at home.
Education, through grade 12	$40,000– $200,000*	Finance a low-budget independent film.	Raise a "child actor" to recoup cost.
College (four years)	$240,000	Rent a 3BR, 2BTH, cntrl air, new mechs, patio, grg.	Make kids leave home at sixteen/get scholarships.

* Vast discrepancy based on the possibility of paying for private schools; the $40,000 assumes public schools and is just the cumulative costs of such items as (for example only; your actual costs may vary) smocks, backpacks, field trip fees, pens, crayons, notebooks, replacement notebooks because the ones you brought home were the wrong kind, foam-core backing for project displays, replacing the school's pet hermit crab that disappeared somewhere in the house over the Christmas break, protractors, annual dance recital costume, tickets and DVD, undelivered Girl Scout cookies or Cub Scout popcorn, piano lessons, gym locker padlocks, SAT coaching, debate team road trips, proms (limo optional), and contributions to the PTA fundraiser, the ski trip fundraiser, the Thanksgiving food drive, and buying the seventy-three candy bars that remained unsold with no time left in the lacrosse team fundraiser. Aren't babies cute?

CHAPTER TWO

Throughout
Your Pregnancy

The Eight Danger Signals

Most of the little complaints and problems of pregnancy do not require that you turn off the ball game; however, today's husband should familiarize himself with the following list of eight dangerous conditions that must be addressed without delay, and without the distractions of play-by-play announcers in the background. If these conditions are ignored, serious long-term damage to your relationship is a very real possibility.

Pay attention to your wife at once if you should notice any of the following conditions:

1. *Glamour-itis.* She is staring down at a magazine and flipping the pages very fast and hard, so that it appears that she isn't actually reading but is most interested in the noise she's making. And on the impact it is having on you.

2. *Lactose Intolerance.* Not the traditional digestive form of lactose intolerance, but a more psychological version. In order to meet the high demands for calcium, lots of milk is recommended. Many women try to make due with ice cream and little chocolate-flavored calcium chews. Others dutifully drink milk until they . . . well, lose

it. Be prepared; she may serve you a pitcher of milk with your dinner, though you seldom drink the stuff. She may mention or imply that she is tired of drinking six to eight glasses of calcium-rich milk every day. She may also follow up with a few comments: "Something wrong with your milk, dear?" "Why aren't you drinking your milk, dear?" In severe cases, she may even pour milk into your beer.

3. *"Fine" Response Syndrome.* She responds to every question or suggestion with "fine," or "sure, fine," or even "fine, that's just fine with me." Fine is seldom fine.

4. *Opthalmoduct Flow.* A clear, odorless fluid that seems to leak from her eyes and is often accompanied by shortness of breath, sobs, and the phrase "you never understand."

5. *Maternal Reflexism.* She returns to her mother's house without telling you. Call and say you didn't mean it, and *do not* say you have no idea what you've done.

6. *Tourella's Syndrome.* Symptomatically related to Tourette's syndrome,

but gender specific, Tourella's is a periodic neurological response in women that is rarely serious. The typical victim, someone who seldom or never swears, gets angry enough to attempt an obscenity. These fledgling efforts are ineffective, awkward, and embarrassing for both parties. For example, when trying to call her husband a shithead, the typical Tourella victim will instead call him a shitty shit. Try not to laugh at her.

7. *Ironic Lyricism.* Her conversational responses tend to be more flowery and poetic than necessary. If you mention you'd like to catch the fight on the tube, she says, "The manly art of pugilism, ah yes, noble fisticuffs. What was it about 'the sweet science,' my darling? Do tell."

8. *Labor and/or Childbirth.* If your wife is in labor or is actually having a baby (see chapter eleven for details), then you should stop ignoring her for a minute and help out. Definitely take the iPod out of your ears. Don't guess at what to do, and don't run and boil towels—just do whatever you wife wants.

The Monthly Prenatal Checkups in Review

Of course, your wife would love it if you could make it to *every* appointment, but after you've weighed yourself on the scales, and read the magazines, and read through the brochures on collecting and storing cord blood (too expensive, don't worry about it), there really isn't that much to do for fun. Anyway, the ob-gyn offices in the hospital are on the same floor as the infertility clinic, so while you may think that you're being perceived as a thoughtful, even doting husband, the other people in the waiting room may be assuming you're there to fill a test tube.

This advice really applies only to the first time around. Later pregnancies, you can usually just hit a couple of appointments and for the rest take the morning off to watch the kids so she can make her appointment. In any case, before you have that excuse, there are some can't-miss appointments and others that aren't worth the price of admission. Here are our capsule reviews:

THE FIRST VISIT: Dull, lots of background medical history, information, basic tests. There are two important reasons to be there: to impress the doctor, and to firmly establish in your wife's mind that you are fully committed to being involved . . . go.

THE SECOND MONTH: Love beat, it's a heartbeat! Now that's entertainment! It may take a few minutes of sliding the walkie-talkie around in the goop on your wife's belly, but when they find that mile-a-minute heartbeat, it's a beautiful thing. So don't miss this one . . . go.

THE THIRD MONTH: Getting a little repetitive already. Wife complains of strange ailments and symptoms and weight gain. Doctor says it's normal; it's to be expected. Thank you, see you next month, good-bye. A definite . . . pass.

THE FOURTH MONTH: More of the same. Your wife keeps trying to come up with something novel to worry about, and the doctor keeps saying it's all perfectly normal, you can't take two aspirin, and don't call me in the morning. Unless you think you should be there to prevent your wife from making up symptoms wholesale (feet swelling like balloons, freckle spread, speaking in tongues) in an effort to have something to worry about . . . pass.

THE FIFTH MONTH: Make sure that you don't miss an ultrasound if your wife is getting one, especially if you've decided to find out the baby's gender, but otherwise . . . pass.

THE SIXTH MONTH: Besides the always-dramatic weigh-in, there isn't much excitement in the middle months. Unless you feel the need to protect yourself from defamation of character during visits to the doctor in this period, you can just be attentive during the at-home recap, and you can safely . . . pass.

THE SEVENTH MONTH: Did you know that, on average, the Asiatic elephant's gestation period is more than twenty months long? The opossum, on the other hand, is pregnant for about twelve days. Share these interesting facts with your wife, but as for the checkup . . . pass.

THE EIGHTH MONTH: Still not too much real news, but now is the time for all good men to come to the service of their wives. The final weeks will be a battle, the approaching due date a bright beacon of hope and fear. It's time to start paying attention, and at the very least, you want to make sure that when you rush into the hospital on the big day, you recognize your obstetrician. Learn her name now . . . go.

THE NINTH MONTH: Now the checks come weekly, but they're also packed with excitement. Is the head down? Can the doctor guess the weight? Does the due date seem right? Should we just head straight on over to the hospital? How early should the baby be taught a second language? As frequently as you can . . . go.

THE SIX-WEEK POSTPARTUM: During labor and childbirth, you, your wife, the obstetrician, and the nice nurse (not the sullen one) bonded into a devoted, affectionate team. Now it's time for a reunion, when you can show off the gem you all produced . . . go.

How Big? Sooo Big!

Tracking the miraculous progress of your unborn child from a blip to a little alien-like ball to a tiny person is fun and educational. When do fingers and toes become apparent? When do eyes open and close? When did Baby learn in utero karate? Here's one man's pet peeve: When you sign up at BabyCenter.com, you get weekly updates, but they always attempt to quantify how big the baby is by comparing it to food. Why food? Why is Baby "the size of a peanut," then "as big as a tangerine," then "an acorn squash," and eventually "a modest watermelon."

Actual quote: "This month your baby is the size of an English Hothouse Cucumber." A what? Are you kidding me? Why English? Why hothouse? Are you saying Baby is long and skinny? That doesn't seem right. They recently compared the baby to a jicama. (That might make a nice name for a girl, by the way.) Maybe pregnant women spend a lot of time in the produce section of the grocery?

I suppose using fruits and vegetables is more appealing than comparing the baby to inanimate objects. That this month your baby is the size of a soap dish or a brick seems a bit demeaning, or even painful. Just relying on adjectives doesn't cut it, either. "This month, your baby is teeny-weeny, but in weeks he will be tiny, and eventually quite small!"

The grocery store approach seems slanted toward women and/or people in the food/restaurant industry. Jicama? So, for the benefit of prefathers who couldn't tell a kumquat from a parsnip, here are a few charts that offer a more relevant metaphorical take on what is going on in there.

End of Month One	Golf ball dimple
Month Two	Golf ball marker
Month Three	Billiard chalk
Month Four	Ping-Pong ball
Month Five	Baseball
Month Six	Softball
Month Seven	Nerf football
Month Eight	Regulation football
Month Nine—Birth	Basketball

Not into sports? All right, how about this.

End of Month One	Size of emergency reset button inside a phone that you need a pen or paperclip to hit
Month Two	Gasket ring of a garden hose
Month Three	2-gigabyte zip drive
Month Four	AA battery
Month Five	Sparkplug
Month Six	Ten-stack of standard poker chips

Month Seven	Pair of balled-up cotton socks
Month Eight	Single standard recessed lighting fixture casing
Month Nine–Birth	Ten-gallon cowboy hat, not including the brim

Here's one for you pragmatic types, broken out by weeks to be more precise. After all, we don't have the same spatial-relations issues our wives seem to have, and may or may not have big issues with the decimal system.

End of 4 weeks	<1 centimeter; <1 gram
8 weeks	1.6 centimeters; 1 gram
12 weeks	5.4 centimeters; 15 grams
16 weeks	11.6 centimeters; 100 grams
20 weeks	25.6 centimeters; 300 grams
24 weeks	30 centimeters; 600 grams
28 weeks	37.6 centimeters; 1,000 grams
32 weeks	42.4 centimeters; 1,700 grams
36 weeks	47.4 centimeters; 2,600 grams
40 weeks–birth	51.3 centimeters; 3,400 grams

High-Tech Pregnant

The incredible pace of technological innovation in the twenty-first century impacts every aspect of our lives, and that includes our experience of pregnancy. Here is a quick guide to some of the latest equipment you'll want during the next ten months.

BREATHALYZER OVULATION PREDICTOR: Dual purpose, this prepregnancy device actually measures when your wife is most fertile simply by reading the hormonal balance in her breath. Change the settings, and it can tell you if you're too drunk to try.

LUB DUB IN DOLBY: This nifty stethoscope allows you to play junior's tiny fast-paced heartbeat through your guitar amp, or any stereo with a standard input.

HOME SONOGRAM: Why wait for the next appointment? This simple device connects to any HD television set so that you can watch your fetus whenever you choose! (Comes with starter pack of twelve bottles of belly goo, enough for up to one hundred viewings.) If you have an iPhone, you can just download the sonogram app, but you'll still need the goo. And don't count on your camera working so well afterward.

WHITE-LIE NONDETECTOR: The lie detector is fairly redundant in most households, since your wife knows full well when you're squirming, fudging, or omitting, but this terrific technical innovation is vital for every couple. It is so finely calibrated that it can distinguish between lies ("Yes, I came straight home from the office.") and white lies ("Of course I want to be at the baby shower.")

MULTIWARMER: Another wonderful dual-purpose item, this single machine provides Baby with gently warmed wipes to make changing time as undisruptive and tranquil as possible, while also providing Dad with luxurious warmed shaving cream! (Manufacturer not responsible for accidents involving product confusion.)

DIAPER GENIE ULTRA: The regular diaper disposal units gather up old diapers in twists of plastic. Fine, but once you have the Ultra (properly and professionally installed), you will be able to dispose of a diaper into a high-pressure vacuum that also sucks in the fifty cubic feet of fetid air around the changing area, wraps the diaper in a triple layer of plastic, and shoots it through induction tubing to a "safe house" as much as fifty yards from your living quarters.

WHAT YOU MAY BE CONCERNED ABOUT

Eating Right

Q. *"I've tried to be supportive and have joined my wife in eating meals that are planned around her special dietary needs during pregnancy. But I'm concerned. Am I doing the right thing?"*

A. Too many perfectly well-intentioned husbands fall into the same trap. What they fail to realize is that a father's special dietary needs are quite different from a pregnant mother's. Your metabolism is different; you are not carrying the child; your needs for iron and minerals are quite different. Simply put, you can eat any crap you like. The big question is, will she let you?

For most expectant fathers, lunch becomes the key meal. After a modest bowl of iron-rich raisin bran for breakfast and with a low-carb spinach salad waiting for you at the end of the day, the midday meal is vital. Off at work, you have a chance to depart from the dietary guidelines you are "sharing." The following recommended foods will help you maintain your health throughout your wife's pregnancy. Remember, these are only recommendations—you should feel free to eat whatever you like, whenever you like, until you make yourself queasy.

THE RAW: Uncooked or very rare foods are risky to your wife for all sorts of hard-to-spell medical reasons, so you'll have to keep them to yourself. But that's no reason to miss out on the thrill of eating oddly textured food with the ever-present danger of food poisoning. Go for it!

Sushi

Steak tartare

Rare steak

Any meat bought from street vendors: hot dogs, red-hot sausages, souvlaki, shish kebab

JUNK: Empty calories are dangerous to the well-balanced, high-protein, high-calcium diet. But whose diet is that? Not yours. Selections from the empty-calorie food group are the perfect accompaniment to a football game, working late, or just getting through the midafternoon doldrums.

Potato chips

Pressed potato product in chiplike form

Doughnuts

Popcorn (buttered, see below)

Candy

Cheese puffs

THE GREASY: Her intestinal balance is easily disturbed; yours can take it. Prove it to her by eating whatever you dang well please, and plenty of it.

Pizza

French fries

Corn dogs

Grilled cheese

Pastrami

THE SPICY: Especially during the period of morning sickness but also throughout pregnancy, heavily spiced foods are exclusively the male province.

Biriyani

Szechuan

Slim Jims

Mexican

THE STINKY: The mere smell of some foods can disturb the pregnant female, so eat 'em at the office, and let your co-workers deal.

Thick soups: mulligatawny, minestrone, split pea

Stinky cheeses: Gorgonzola, Saga blue, etc.

Peanut butter

Wiener schnitzel and sauerkraut

Other Dietary Restrictions

FOOD ADDITIVES: Fresh fruits and vegetables, simple fish and chicken dishes, locally baked breads, rice, and homemade soup are safe. So when you're on your own? Make sure that you have a plastic wrapper or two to dispose of at the end of every meal.

MERCURY: Remember Mercury Morris? The Dolphins' running back under those great Don Shula teams? With Jim Kiick and Larry Csonka? Probably before your time, but think about it: Have there ever been three more poetically named running backs in one era, much less on one team? Mercury, Kiick, Csonka. If Charles Dickens had written *Semi-Tough* . . . but we digress. Fish apparently have too much mercury in them.

ALCOHOL: While discouraged for the mom-to-be, beer is an essential part of any future father's daily intake. It has vitamins B_6 and B_{12}, nutrients that are vital to your immunological system or bone formation or something like that. In any case, we recommend a good cheap local beer—fresh and served uncomfortably cold. Two or three taken internally each evening will provide a salubrious spiritual cushion.

CAFFEINE: Not recommended for her, but for you? What better way to jumpstart your day? And your body needs caffeine, especially during times of stress and exhaustion. It would be best if you were to drink a whole lot of coffee, pretty much all day long, along with the occasional Red Bull, but caffeine can also be found in smaller amounts in tea, in some sodas (which also supply large amounts of vital sugar), and in chocolate. If it interferes with your ability to sleep . . . well, that's just good practice for what's to come.

BREAKDOWN OF YOUR WIFE'S WEIGHT GAIN		BREAKDOWN OF YOUR WIFE'S 7 LB. MATERNAL FAT	
Baby, etc. (placenta, amniotic fluid, uterine enlargement	12.75 lbs.	Milk fats	2.75 lbs.
Maternal breast tissue	1 lb.	Eating for two	1.5 lbs.
Maternal blood volume, fluids in maternal tissue	5.75 lbs.	Tasti D-Lite	.75 lbs.
Maternal fat (see adjoining column for complete details)	7 lbs.	Office birthday cakes it would have been impolite to refuse	.5 lbs.
Total average gain	**26.5 lbs.**	Just-one-bites from husband's desserts	2.5 lbs.
		Unfair, inexplicable, punishment-from-God weight gain	1.75 lbs.
		Ben & Jerry's	1.5 lbs.
		High-salt, high-fat, bagged junk foods too embarrassing to mention by name	1.75 lbs.
		Total 7 lb. gain*	**13 lbs.**

*The difference between the seven-pound average maternal fat gain and the thirteen pounds of maternal fat we calculated cannot be explained. It just kinda snuck up on us.

When Not to Call the Practitioner

You should, of course, familiarize yourself with the symptoms and problems that you should immediately report to your doctor—severe abdominal pain, spotting or bleeding, severe headache, visual disturbances, fainting, dizziness, chills, or fever. However, it is also important to know what symptoms do *not* require immediate attention. By studying these symptoms, you can save yourself pointless and time-consuming jaunts to the local hospital.

- Sudden or severe crankiness
- Gradual enlarging of the belly area
- Everything going too smoothly
- A sudden increase in thirst, swelling or puffiness in the hands, severe headaches, fever, fainting, dizziness, sudden weight gain, nausea, or visual disturbances when they occur in the father
- Crying during sappy made-for-TV movies, when sad songs are played on the radio, or when there are really cute kids on commercials
- Generally worried
- Need for makeup tips to accentuate "healthy glow"
- Sudden worry about the state of public schools in your area
- Tivo keeps choosing to record shows you have no interest in
- Your inability to feel the fetal movement even though your wife insists you ought to be able to
- Occurrences of any unusual symptoms in a woman you don't know but is a Facebook friend of your cousin and now that she thinks about it maybe she does have that unusual symptom
- Doctor gave an odd-numbered due date, and your wife's always hated odd numbers
- Constant clumsiness and spilling of drinks
- Inability to decide on a name, especially during the first trimester
- A foot that's gone to sleep
- Inability to find anything good to watch on TV or the DVR or the Internet

Exercise

Q. *"We've gotten all sorts of information about exercise for my wife: the Kegel, dromedary droops, and pelvic-tilt exercises. What is the right form of exercise for a pregnant father?"*

A. A good rule of thumb is that the easiest exercise is no exercise at all. Occasionally thinking to yourself that you ought to get started on some program but then thinking you don't look *that* bad and realizing that a pretty good hockey game is on TV may not do you any good, but it sure is relaxing.

Still, if you do want to get in shape to help your wife through her pregnancy and to prepare yourself for the rigors of early fatherhood, there are some specific exercises that can help. Remember, you're pregnant, too! So start slowly, don't strain, taper off during the last trimester, and avoid contact sports like football, rugby, and extreme cage fighting.

WIFE CATCHING: Stand in a relaxed position, feet spread slightly, knees bent. Then have an assistant tip a double mattress in your direction. Catch the mattress, then lead it out of the room without breaking any furniture. Repeat, and when you reach a high success level, you'll be well prepared to help your wife maneuver in crowded restaurants in her ninth month.

LABOR COACH'S NECK TILT: To prepare yourself for a long and sleepless labor: Sit in a comfortable position. Allow your eyelids to fall slowly over your eyes, and tilt your neck to one side; then suddenly jerk your head straight up, open your eyes, and say, "Yes, honey?" Repeat fifteen or twenty times daily.

BASIC KEGEL EXERCISES: Join your wife when she does her Kegels. Lie on your back with your head supported and your knees up. Let your arms lie flat at your sides. Slowly tense and then relax the muscles in your penis. Do at least twenty-five repetitions. It may not have any particular benefit, but it's a hell of a lot more pleasant than most exercises. And no, you don't have to stretch out first.

STROLL-UPS: Hold a twenty-pound weight under one arm. Stoop down, bending at the knees unless you don't want to, and using your one free hand change the battery in your watch, stand, and repeat. (This exercise will prepare you for the process of opening or closing a "portable" stroller while holding Baby in one arm.)

RUNNING: Sit up suddenly from a comfortable seat. Raise your left arm, pulling your hand outward to reveal your watch. Tilt your head toward your left wrist and say, "Oh, shoot, I've gotta run." Get up and leave, making sure your right hand has opened completely and left the beer on the bar.

What Not to Do

Q. *"She's pregnant, but she won't lie down. My wife is still working, jogging, everything. Isn't a pregnant woman not supposed to lift anything, or do anything?"*

A. Unless her doctor advises otherwise, pregnancy should not prevent your wife from engaging in any of her ordinary activities. Work, sex, even noncontact sports are all okay. There are, nonetheless, some strictures. The following activities are to be avoided—as much as possible—as soon as she knows she is pregnant:

Limbo dancing

Bungee cord jumping

Tournament Twister

Rewiring your home using a do-it-
yourself handbook

Slam dancing

Playing box lacrosse

Asbestos removal

Driving in demolition derbies

Touring sites of nuclear accidents

Sword swallowing

Riding the NASA centrifuge to test
g-force endurance

Bear baiting

Freedom fighting as a mercenary in
Central America

Time travel

Quitting Smoking Now

Q. *"I'm trying to quit smoking so my wife and the baby won't have to deal with my secondhand smoke, but I just can't seem to break the habit."*

A. Listen up. You're eating what you want. You're still knocking off a few brews each evening. You're keeping your local Starbucks in business. Shouldn't you give up something in the spirit of solidarity? Sure, your father didn't have to quit smoking, but that was then, this is now. It is the least you can do, and living longer isn't a bad side benefit. Watching your kids grow up will give anyone a refreshed desire to stick around for as long as possible, just to see how it all comes out.

Now, outwrestling the nicotine monkey is never easy, and with the on-coming responsibilities of family—the accelerating financial demands, the endless emotional stress, the constant demands on your time—well, frankly, you deserve to sit back and enjoy some real tobacco satisfaction. Don't do it! Put it out right now. You *can* quit—you can handle it all, and without your thin white pals.

The key to quitting is to determine which aspect of smoking appeals to you the most. Is it the nicotine? Or is it oral gratification? Or just something to do with your hands? Think about it. What do you miss the most? After you decide why smoking appeals to you, just look on the following chart for a simple, health-ful substitute. After you use the substitute to wean yourself from the noxious weed, then you can work on kicking the substitutes. If you can't, just remember: Scientists have proven that cigarettes are *not* dangerous to your health. (Until you light them on fire and suck on them.)

APPEALING ASPECTS OF SMOKING	SUBSTITUTE
Effects of nicotine	Try the patch, chewing tobacco, snorting snuff.
Something to do with my hands	Eat Pixy Stix candy all day long; learn card tricks; grow facial hair and smooth it a lot; scratch privates frequently.
Morning headaches	Drink too much, especially warm gin and/or tequila.
Enjoyment of dependency	Take up another addiction: caffeine, gambling, fantasy sports.
Carbon monoxide	Inhale automobile fumes, either by taking walks near heavy traffic or in the privacy of your own garage.
Yellow-stained hands and mustache	Use food coloring.
Dizziness and nausea	Spin in fast circles.
Pleasure derived from handing money to local merchants for something that does me no good whatsoever	Buy lottery tickets.
Smelling bad	Minimize toothbrushing
Looking cool	Grow sideburns a little longer; get some serious tattoo work; never wear sweaters; get an eye patch.

CHAPTER THREE

The First Month

What Your Wife May Look Like

Throughout the first month, her eyes will be agleam, because intuitively she already knows. Her cheeks may be flushed, as she probably has a pretty good idea which night it was, too. She chooses the clothes she knows you like. Healthy glow? Yes, but alternating with the unhealthy greenish glow of morning sickness.

What Your Wife
Will Be Complaining About

BEFORE SHE KNOWS

- Exhaustion

- You

- Not being pregnant after all these months of trying

- Her college roommate who gets pregnant every time her husband looks at her

- Home pregnancy testing kits—kinda pricey and embarrassing to buy

- That everyone else in the world seems to be pregnant; "what if we can't get pregnant?"

- That you don't believe her when she says she "just feels pregnant"

- Her voracious sexual appetite, or . . .

AFTER SHE KNOWS

- Her complete lack of interest in sex

- Heartburn and indigestion, flatulence and bloating

- Heartburn and indigestion, flatulence and bloating in *you*, and what's your excuse?

- Why last month, or even the month before would have been a better time to get pregnant, because it's miserable being pregnant in the winter (or summer, spring, or fall, as the case may be), and this bad timing is somehow all your responsibility

- That the hospital won't let you sign up for their childbirth preparedness classes until you're seven months' pregnant

- Aversions to certain foods—especially chicken soup right after you make a huge vatful

- That the romantic trip to Venice must happen now—when she feels horrible—or be delayed for a decade or so

- Stretch marks (not actual stretch marks, just the *concept* of stretch marks)

- Emotional highs and lows, fear, ecstasy, anxiety, and elation, often all at the same time

A Couple of Things to Say to Let Her Know You're Caring, Sensitive, and Up On the Required Reading

What your wife is expecting you to read is a whole stack of books. (And, sadly, this one doesn't count, unless she hasn't read it. You might get away with it.) In any case, to save you the trouble of reading all those thick guides, we have read (all right, skimmed) dozens of books about childbirth and pregnancy and gleaned a few interesting and relevant facts for you to memorize and use. Don't worry about getting caught; if she presses you for details, it's a simple matter to say, "Gee, I can't remember exactly where I read that—I've been through so many books now."

Unlike many other sections of this volume, the "Couple of Things to Say..." are completely real. You may simply be trying to make a good impression, but, as it happens, you could actually learn something along the way.

1. "One early symptom of pregnancy is Montgomery's tubercles, sebaceous glands in the areola of the nipple that become prominent. Shall I check for them?"

2. "Among the battery of tests at your first visit to the ob-gyn will be the rubella titer, which tests for immunity to German measles, so it doesn't matter that you lost your record of childhood immunizations."

3. "Margaret Mead's research in New Guinea found that in some societies boils are considered a typical symptom of pregnancy."

What to Buy This Month

Your little bundle of joy will cost you a little bundle before you even get to take it home from the hospital. To help you organize and realistically assess your financial needs in the coming months, we have broken down all the necessary purchases into a set of monthly lists.

If you are superstitious, or just uncomfortable about buying things for the baby before the actual birth, then don't. There is no reason you can't buy everything you need after the baby has arrived safely (although the credit card company may get panicky and start asking stores to verify your identity).

ESTIMATED COSTS, MONTH ONE

Basics: $78

Basics plus extras: $300,078

Basics

Home pregnancy test kit

The real *What to Expect When You're Expecting*

Dr. Spock (the pediatrician, not the first officer)

A baby name book

Vitamins—for you

Extras

A home in the suburbs

Anything listed in the "What to Buy" section of later months, because you can't wait until you actually *know* that you're pregnant

All the selfish luxury items you won't dare buy once you're a family man—ride-on mower, iPad, pizza oven, single malt Scotch, nice ties, season tickets, monogrammed poker chips

The Minefield: A Guide to the Wrong Gifts for Your Pregnant Wife

We won't even deal with the eternally wrong gifts—vacuum cleaners, cash, unexpected pets, tickets to your favorite events, rain checks for something-to-come, and so forth. We'll focus on the mistakes that could happen when, right

in the middle of your pregnancy, along comes one of those always inconvenient holidays, anniversaries, or birthdays. With ten months of expecting, you surely won't be able to dodge them all. Oh, and while we're thinking of it, don't forget a "pushing" gift for Mom, which should be ready when Baby arrives.

1. *Wines or liquor*

Hello? Last call for alcohol was months ago. The only possible exception would be if you know that she is looking forward to celebrating the end of pregnancy/nursing with some special bottle or a very tall frozen concoction.

2. *Baby clothes, toys, and other baby stuff*

She is not the baby. Don't confuse the two. She is still your wife, and a person. Rattles, teddy bears, onesies, safety latches, strollers, swings, 529k contributions . . . none of these qualify as a gift for her. Parental devotion is nice. Save it for some other time.

3. *Jogging stroller*

Even if she expressed interest, you better be very sure that she won't take this as a "looking forward to seeing you get back in shape" gift. The same goes for anything exercise related.

4. *Unexpected pet*

Okay, we already mentioned this, but here it is for emphasis. What are you going to do with an ocelot when she points out the inherent irresponsibility of having a barely nonferal creature in the house with an infant?

5. *Vacation trip*
Now, this could be okay, but you better be sure. Especially if you're planning on a "leave the baby with Grandma" vacation for two. You're supposed to be embracing family life, not running away from it.

6. *Rain checks*
It might seem cute to draw up little coupons for future vacations or extravagances, but it's really not a gift at all, is it?

7. *Clothes with implications*
And what clothes don't have some implication? No matter how much your wife loves being pregnant (some really do), she is bound to have mixed feelings about the state of her body, and the last thing she wants is to contemplate either accepting the changes or the fight to resist them or what you think is appropriate mommy-wear. All this assumes you aren't contemplating the purchase of anything in the realm of the sexy nightie.

8. *Tools, stereo, TV equipment*
Who are you kidding? No boy toy,

unless maybe a DVR, is going to make her TV viewing experience better. But if you do get one, you better not fill it up with old ball games or *Deadliest Catch*.

9. *Things you can't really afford*
Once, stretching beyond the usual budget might have sent the message that you loved her SO much, but now it just shows you aren't being sensible. Keep your receipts.

WHAT YOU MAY BE CONCERNED ABOUT

Sex During Pregnancy

Q. *"Okay, we're not even sure she's pregnant yet, but I'm worried already, so what about sex during pregnancy?"*

A. The approach of fatherhood is a time full of tension, anxiety, and self-doubt. Sex can be the perfect way to relax and escape the pressures. Furthermore, there is no medical or physiological reason to prevent you from engaging in a full sexual life. However, like most men, you may feel uncomfortable about cheating on your wife, so sex is out.

Now might be a good time to take up a diverting hobby like collecting stamps, building plastic models, or watching too much TV. Keep yourself busy and you'll forget all about those troublesome urges, just like the old Boy Scout manual said.

Q. Tippling for Two

"My wife had a few drinks before we knew she was pregnant. Could this be a big problem?"

A. Probably not. A better indicator of a problem is when the father has a *lot* of drinks *after* he finds out they're pregnant. That's a big problem. As for the young mother, certainly drinking during pregnancy is not recommended, but a few drinks are still statistically very unlikely to cause a problem for the baby. Stop worrying. A generation ago, midafternoon martinis were standard fare to help pregnant moms relax and unwind. Remember, in France, even very young children drink large quantities of wine with every meal, and look at France. On second thought, maybe cutting back a little wouldn't hurt.

Q. Genetic Counseling

"They've suggested genetic counseling for us. What's up with that? And is there any way to cheat on the tests?"

A. Depending on your age, your wife's age, your ethnic heritage, or your desire to spend lots of money on elective (uninsured) medical advice and testing, you may find yourself undergoing prenatal genetic counseling. "Advanced age" is a nice piece of wordsmithing to make it sound good, but it is not. It is well known that serious issues become statistically more likely in older parents.

Counseling, combined with a variety of tests, can establish the likelihood of many specific fetal development issues.

And the whole thing can make you feel lousy.

First of all, what a guilt trip. There's nothing quite as powerless as thinking about the state of your DNA. What are you supposed to do about it? First, there is the simple matter of figuring out the roots of your family tree. One-sixteenth Cherokee? Two or maybe three thirty-seconds Ashkenazi Jew? Then there are the various failings the flesh is heir to. No amount of your diet and exercise will delete Uncle Wilbur, who drank, or Aunt Patricia, who had "spells." They are all evidence of potential weakness in your procreative stature. Skin cancer? Breast Cancer? Heart disease? Diabetes? Simple-mindedness? Mental retardation? Frizzy hair? As you are quizzed on all these possibilities, if your family is properly repressed, you may be racking your memory banks for the vaguest rumors of ancestors from the 1940s, '50s, and '60s.

Unraveling all the factors, recessive genes, fractional ancestry, and so forth is complicated, even if you did pretty well in tenth-grade biology. Don't be afraid to ask about what you don't understand. There are no stupid questions. Well, on the other hand, before you ask, there is no DNA test to see whether you have been bitten by a radioactive spider, and in any case it would not give you the proportionate strength of anything.

But there is good news! Here are some male genetic issues that are certainly inherited traits, but which pose no specific fetal threat. Better yet, your baby daughters are immune. These are behavioral issues that will only manifest themselves in male children upon maturity:

1. Snoring

2. Inability or unwillingness to throw away distinctly worn-out underwear

3. Waistline dislocation: Often appearing in early middle age, this condition allows men to continue wearing the same waist-size pants simply by displacing the "waist" below the accumulation of nondisplaced beer- and snack-related expansion.

4. Construction hypnosis: Um. Big machines go, make things, change Earth. Mmm.

5. Gnarly toes

6. Terpsichoraphobia (fear of ballroom dancing)

7. SDS (snoring denial syndrome)

8. Testosterone-fueled road rage: Even mild-mannered citizens feel the biochemical surges that seek vengeance for being passed on the right when it should be perfectly obvious that the guys ahead of you are the problem.

9. The yips: Drive for show, putt for dough.

10. Chore accumulation syndrome: CAS affects literally millions of men each weekend. There was going to be a walk for the cure, but we put it off until after football season, and then it was too cold.

11. Obtruding nasal cilia: In laymen's terms, this is excessive unmanaged nose hair.

12. Manual transmission fetish: Though technology has completely eliminated all possible rationales not to drive an automatic, the notion of "real driving" remains a vital source of pride.

Genetic-Issues Pop Quiz

That's right, a quiz for you, the potential pop. This simple set of questions can be used by a medical professional to determine whether you are at risk for any of the male genetic issues above, or even some more obscure conditions. Fill it out and bring it with you to your appointment.

1. Have you ever painted your face with your school colors? Painted your torso? Anything else?

2. Do you avoid parallel parking where there are people watching? Conversely, do you seek out difficult parking situations, or enjoy driving backward down long driveways?

3. Have you ever considered brewing your own beer?

4. Do you spend an inordinate amount of time picking up sticks off your lawn?

5. Do tattoos cover more than 40 percent of your epidermis? Twenty percent? And do you have any tattoos that the human resources department asks that you keep covered during work hours?

6. Which is more expensive, your stereo or your wife's car? How did you manage that?

7. Is your carbon footprint way bigger than average?

8. Can you do a pretty fair impression of a trumpeting elephant? A donkey? The Aflac duck?

9. Do you own two or more of the following: a posthole digger, a voltmeter, a bench grinder, a three-hook fence stretcher, a lawn edge cutter, safety goggles, a hazmat suit, or a ball-peen hammer?

10. Have you ever checked out the cost of a used backhoe?

11. Are military push-ups part of your daily regimen?

12. Have you ever driven more than 120 miles per hour?

13. Have you ever scraped mold off food and then eaten it?

14. Have you ever considered trying to stitch up an injury yourself?

15. Who would win in a fight, Voltron or Optimus Prime?

16. Do you insist that your wife be the tooth fairy?

17. Does your barber know your name?

18. Do you own a martini shaker?

19. Have you ever had to put anything larger than an insect out of its misery?

20. When you were a kid, how many windows did you break?

Q. Gender Preference

"I foolishly expressed a slight preference for a boy. Now how do I convince my wife that I won't hate a girl?"

A. All is not lost. There are two tactics that might work.

The first plan is to say, "I only said that because I thought you had a slight preference for a boy; I would actually much prefer a girl." This lie must then be followed by a full-fledged propaganda campaign: Buy pink booties, talk only about girls' names you like, call the baby "she" at all times, and mention that you heard that girls are much easier to toilet train, which is true, by the way.

The other plan is to claim that you didn't say it at all, that in fact the cat said it. Be sincerely amazed that the cat talked. Wonder if there's someone you should call. The newspapers? The Humane Society? The president? Don't budge an inch, and eventually your wife may think that you are actually mentally disturbed and under too much pressure. Though not a long-term solution, it may give you enough time for things to cool down.

Judging by these solutions, of course, the best thing is to avoid the situation at all cost. Get your answer down pat now: You want a healthy, happy baby—boy or girl is the furthest thing from your mind. Maintain this attitude without wavering and you'll be all right. And don't feel bad. Let's face it, all men really have a slight preference for a boy, and all women really have a slight preference for a girl. It's a matter of sociobiology. First of all, we're all egoists, so replicating ourselves is job number one. Men also want someone to toss a baseball with, not someone to play volleyball with; but, more than anything, it all comes back to your basic inability to understand women. No matter how cute daughters are, you know that someday she will baffle you with her feminine mystique. In that sense, hoping for a boy is just as normal as hoping for a baby who speaks English. You want to understand what they're saying, right?

Q. Weight Gain

"How much is the right amount? I hear conflicting information."

A. Weight gain is inevitable during pregnancy. In fact, it is advisable! How much? Well, you shouldn't try to actually match your wife's gain. Don't go overboard, but putting on a pound or so every couple of weeks is something to aim for. The idea of dieting or doing more exercise and actually losing weight while your wife is putting on her twenty to thirty (or more) pounds poses definite health risks. The risks are mainly of being smacked, locked out of the house, or just glared at. Here's something not to say: "A couple of weeks more at this rate and we'll weigh the same thing!"

Toxoplasmosis

Q. *"I've heard that I may be able . . . we may have to get rid of our cats because of the danger of toxoplasmosis."*

A. If you've been dying for an opportunity to get rid of the mangy soulless felines, read your wife the paragraph below; if you actually like cats, skip to the paragraph that follows it.

Cat feces and raw meat often carry the parasitic organism known as *Toxoplasma gondii*. It causes a disease that can be very mild—often going unnoticed in those who have its low-grade fever, swollen glands, and rash. However, the disease poses a serious threat to the fetus of a pregnant woman. It can cause permanent damage, illness, or even death. Cats should be tested, but in most cases simply sent away. You should also avoid contact with other people's cats, and avoid gardening in soil that cats may have used as a litter box.

The odds are high that if you have cats, or eat raw meat regularly,* you long ago contracted the disease and are now immune. A simple, but not-covered-by-your-annoying-HMO, test at the doctor's office can establish this for certain. Of the very small number of women who contract the disease, 60 percent don't pass it on to their fetus, and two-thirds of affected babies show no ill effects anyway. Also, damage is unlikely to occur in the first trimester. Just have your cat tested for an active infection, then keep it indoors, away from mice, birds, or other cats. And when pregnant, a woman should let her husband deal with the litter box.

You can dump the cats or keep them. In either case, you should avoid eating any raw or very rare meat. And it almost goes without saying that you certainly shouldn't eat raw cat.

* Who the heck eats raw meat regularly?

CHAPTER FOUR

The Second Month

What Your Wife May Look Like

Toward the end of the second month, she will wear, for the last time ever, that great pair of jeans she's had since college. She may think she's showing, since her belly isn't completely flat. Don't argue the point. Healthy glow? None—complete takeover by the unhealthy greenish glow of morning sickness.

What Your Wife
Will Be Complaining About

- Exhaustion
- You
- Morning sickness
- Midmorning sickness
- Afternoon sickness
- Dusk sickness
- Late-evening sickness
- Whoever named it morning sickness
- The "reassuring" pregnancy books that terrify her because she keeps skipping ahead to the "what could go wrong" sections
- Iron supplements and the inevitable constipation they cause
- That she wants to ask the doctor about the terrifying condition pre-eclampsia but isn't sure how to pronounce it
- The sudden realization that the child could inherit *your* nose
- How she's dying to tell everyone she's pregnant
- Your mother, who has happily informed you she hasn't thrown out any of her three-decade-old baby clothes, and that the trunk is in the mail
- Fear that the dog will be jealous
- Emotional highs and lows, fear, ecstasy, anxiety, and elation, often all at the same time

A Couple of Things to Say to Let Her Know You're Caring, Sensitive, and Up On the Required Reading

1. "That morning sickness is rough, honey, but at least you don't have Hyperemesis gravidarum, the rare condition of severe and unremitting vomiting that must be treated with antiemetic drugs. Right?"

2. "Nitrates and nitrites in food can become potentially harmful nitrosamines, so we'll avoid eating cured or commercially prepared hams, bacon, sausage, luncheon meats, smoked fish, Chinese salt-dried fish, and raw or smoked salmon or shad."

3. "Did you know that by the sixth week of gestation, the anterior and posterior horns differentiate in the spinal cord of the fetus? I didn't even know babies came with horns!"

What to Buy This Month

It's never too soon to begin indulging in frivolities and all the things you remember from wherever you last saw actual babies in action. If it looks useful, buy it. If it looks cute, buy it. You, my friend, are a dad-to-be. You have a right to these things. Your wife can't question your devotion or fiscal wisdom.

ESTIMATED COSTS, MONTH TWO

Basics: $200
Basics plus extras: $350

Basics
Booties
Bicycle baby seat
Bicycling helmet
Busy box, to hang in crib
Crib mobile

Electric bowl (keeps gruel warm)
Jolly Jumper (actually, these are hard to find, since they are obviously so unsafe—try eBay)
Onesies: the adorable little one-piece underwear with the snaps in the crotch
Port-a-Play: toys that you suspend over infants for batting practice
Silver spoon
Teething rings
DVD of *Dumbo*

Extras
Baby shaders, to attach to the inside of car windows to protect the baby's eyes from the sun
Eton suit or tiny white lace gown, depending on what you're expecting

High-contrast black-and-white crib mobile

Mountain stroller: four-by-four stroller with high underbody clearance and independent four-wheel suspension

Euro-stroller: Every few years there is some new, funky stroller from Europe that looks like nothing you've ever seen and costs more than you ever imagined; see buying guide below.

The Right Stroll

Your choice of which stroller to purchase says a lot about your commitment to parenting. There is no more public and conspicuous item, and it declares exactly how much your baby's comfort and safety mean to you. But you don't have to feel peer pressure. Go ahead. Get the basic model: simple, lightweight, functional. The price is right, no? Just don't forget in your considerations to add in the price of an entirely new, much more impressive stroller that you will be back to buy three months after the baby arrives. Yes, it's a status symbol. But who doesn't like status? Hey, that's just how we stroll, Baby.

Strollers have come a long way in the past few years. In the first edition of this book, for example, the price of a good stroller was estimated at $150. The next edition was $300. Now it's easy to spend $500. Thought: Stop investing in mu-

nicipal bonds or real estate! Buy yourself a warehouse full of high-end strollers and in five years you'll be sitting on a gold mine!

The main source of the inflation is imports from Germany, Sweden, Norway, even France. Do the Europeans actually use these stylish and incredibly expensive strollers? We suspect they just use old hand-me-down prams and laughingly manufacture more and more elaborate, aerodynamic, and ergonomic baby conveyors to sell to Americans for $1,200. Just like they sell us hefty BMW and Volvo sedans while they all drive cars you could park in a walk-in closet. Or maybe the stroller companies are like Häagen-Dazs and Frusen Glädjé, ice cream made in places like New Jersey and Long Island but given mysteriously foreign names as the quickest marketing shortcut to "quality" ever invented.

But since nothing is too good for your baby, here are some features to look for when you take out a loan to get yourself a stroller.

1. *Antilock brakes:* Smoother transitions help prevent minor accidents.

2. *Tailgating heel bumpers:* Nothing's more embarrassing than accidentally taking your eye off the flow of traffic ahead and nipping the heels of innocent pedestrians. These special bumpers minimize discomfort and potential damage to their Achilles tendons.

3. *On-board bottle warmer:* What could be more convenient? The optional setting will also keep Mom's decaf skim latte piping hot.

4. *One-hand fold and store:* You'll want to look for a stroller that can collapse easily with one hand so you can keep the baby tucked under the other arm. Of course, now that it is folded up into its most compact configuration, you will also want a small forklift to get it up and into the back of your minivan.

5. *In-carriage DVD player/video port:* These are swivels to allow a parent to view streaming Netflix once napping has commenced.

6. *Air conditioning:* The benefits of "some fresh air" are greatly overstated. Why not take that fresh air and filter and dehumidify it before delivering it inside the hermetically sealed carriage at a constant 72 degrees? (Of course, the plebeians at the park may think you've got an immunologically challenged "Boy in the Plastic Bubble," but that's their problem.)

7. *Hover!* The hovercraft technology guarantees the smoothest ride, and better yet, because the stroller never touches the ground, no germs can travel off the street, up the wheels, across the under-carriage, and onto the handlebar, which Baby may accidentally touch with her gloved hands!

Or What a Friend of Yours May Be Concerned About

Q. *"This friend of mine, not me, was wondering if there's any way of knowing whether the baby is definitely his. More specifically, is there a way of establishing this without letting his wife know there is any doubt, because, as you can imagine, such a doubt could be extremely destructive to a relationship in and of itself, if you know what I mean."*

A. Whew. You're in big trouble. If you can't find out, you'll be racked with doubts and anxieties. If you try to find out—well, right or wrong, if she finds out that you were trying to find out, it's over. One thing for sure: If you're not sure, and you're suddenly invited to appear on a daytime talk show . . . don't go!

We guess you just have to hope that your suspicions are not correct. Sorry, that's the best we are going to offer. It's certainly possible that there is a blood test or some other kind of test that could be done in conjunction with amniocentesis, but even in the name of research we wouldn't dare start asking questions about it. Get serious. A guy goes around asking those questions, claiming it's research, and before you know it, someone overhears, passes it on, and boom, marriage over. In this territory, even hypothetical questions are just too dangerous. Sorry. In fact, I wouldn't even linger on this page too long if I were you.

The Interim Name

Q. *"We're pregnant; this is fabulous. There's nothing my wife and I would rather do than sit around talking about him, or is it her? What should we call our fetus? 'It' seems so impersonal."*

A. Within your wife, a new life has sprung into potentiality, and for the next nine months you will be obsessed with charting the development of the fetus into a baby, planning and sacrificing as you enter a new life as parents of . . . him, her, or it.

For some, the answer is simply to rely on women's intuition. Whatever your wife's hunch is—boy or girl—just assume she's right. (In case you haven't already picked up on this theme, assuming your wife is right is one of the central tenets of this guide.) If she doesn't have a guess, don't worry—complete strangers will soon begin taking one look at your wife and telling you, "It's a girl because she's carrying low and wide," or "It's a boy because

her skin looks so great." So just find a consensus and go with that gender.

If you're afraid of guessing wrong, creating false expectations, or possibly offending your unborn child, you might want to give it a nickname. It seems that every couple comes up with their own unique moniker. One couple we know went with Herbie for reasons known only to themselves. Junior is popular, but does seem to imply a boy. Another called their baby-to-be The Peanut, based on a pregnancy book's description of a two-month-old fetus. Still another well-organized couple picked a male and a female name and spoke of "him/her" and "Megan/Daniel." (Actually, she/he was Megan/Daniel until the fourth month, when the husband had second thoughts and started calling him/her Megan/Charles, while his wife stuck with Megan/Daniel; and then after the amnio results determined that they were carrying a boy, they settled on Michael, but that's probably a whole lot more complicated than you wanted to know. Although, perhaps, you should also know that when he was born, Michael became Jonathan, and still is.)

So feel free to call Baby-to-be whatever you like, whatever makes you comfortable, with the possible exception of cute diminutives of the scientific names. If you do fall into calling your baby-to-be Fetey, or Embry, keep it to yourselves.

Avoiding Couvade Syndrome

Q. *"I'm terrified that I may contract this Couvade syndrome thing and get morning sickness, retain water, and have nightmares about stretch marks. How can I avoid a sympathetic pregnancy?"*

A. Couvade syndrome is a psychosomatic condition also known as sympathetic pregnancy. Its male victim suffers from all the symptoms of pregnancy. In the most serious cases, his belly will actually swell. In less serious cases, he will simply suffer from morning sickness and general crankiness.

Common sense tells us that the best way to avoid a sympathetic pregnancy is not to be too sympathetic. For most men, this comes naturally, but many may need to work on it. At the first signs of morning sickness in yourself, don't panic, but do take positive steps. Explain to your wife what's going on. When she understands that Couvade syndrome is a legitimate medical condition, she will laugh with spiteful delight, but later on she will more than likely understand that right now you just need a little time to be cold, distant, and detached. If you can't absent yourself completely, try to ease off from being sympathetic gradually. Stop listening attentively to her complaints; promise to do little errands and forget them; and when she reads sections of pregnancy books to you, comment on the prose style, or question her pronunciation of a word.

If your symptoms persist, you may even need to play little pranks on her: Tamper with the bathroom scale, set all the clocks in the house back two hours, or replace her shoes with a pair a whole size smaller. There's no end to the fun you can have, and afterward you'll both share a good laugh.

Couvade syndrome is unfortunate, but until there's a cure, at least it's nice to know that there are positive steps you can take to minimize its effects.

College

Q. *"How can I ensure that our baby is accepted by the college of his or her choice?"*

A. By the second month, the initial feelings of joy and/or panic will have worn off, and the time comes for reflection. While your wife isn't even showing, the seismic shift in life is impossible to ignore. Expecting a child is a wondrous, joyful, and awe-inspiring experience. With conception came a rush of new feelings, among them an overwhelming sense of responsibility. Parents-to-be not only need to tend to their babies' health and well-being but also need to educate them, instill pride in them, and most of all, give them every possible edge on the competition.

Prepared parents know that and have already given their strategy some thought. Savvy parents know, for example, *when* to give birth. They've aimed for the time of the year that will avoid those unfortunate school year "cusps" that make their child the youngest in their class. You want to be in the older half of any given class because in those early years even a matter of months can create a perception of maturity or advancement that is really only a factor of time.

If you didn't think of that, it's water breaking under the bridge. But don't let another opportunity pass you by. Preparation begins in the womb. If you wait until your baby is born to begin the educational process, they'll probably be okay, just a few steps behind the other kids. What to do? Don't let your fetus spend nine months staring at the uterine walls! Here are just a few ideas:

- *Womb tunes.* All parents play Mozart to their developing fetus. Avoid the clichés and broaden the baby's musical palate. Any classical music is appropriate, with the possible exception of Wagnerian opera, which might just scare the baby out of ever coming out. If you are less interested in your child's depth of knowledge, and more interested in assuring that he is considered cool, you could choose to play Dylan, Lou Reed, Ry Cooder, and blues guitar legends like Albert King and the Reverend Gary Davis. Just don't forget that when

cool kids become teenagers, they hate their parents. Maybe a slightly nebbish teenager is better in the long run? To that end, the most sensible approach is to begin with Gregorian chant and other early music and work chronologically through baroque all the way to the work of modernists like Copland and John Cage. This will give your unborn child a sense of the historical continuity and development of musical composition.

- *Talk to your womb.* Social skills are just as important as cognitive ones. Make small talk. Establish a sense of propriety and decorum. Speak firmly, with conviction, but offer support. Remember, love *and* limits. Kids—and fetuses (feti?)—may test you, but they want to know that you are confident and in charge.

- *Buy the right toys for the fetus.* The Press 'n' Play Alphabet, for example, is a wonderful learning tool. These hand-carved wood letters can be pushed against Mommy's tummy to allow the baby-to-be to begin recognizing his letters.

- *Buy motivational tapes.* In addition to the basic repertoire of literary books on tape, there are also many instructive motivational tapes specifically for the unborn. We especially recommend *Fetus Self-Improvement: Being Born Is Just the Beginning!* which provides gentle music imbued with simple, almost subliminal messages that will make for a better baby: "Don't cry too much," "When it is dark outside, we sleep," and "Let's make toilet training a priority."

Maternity Fashion

Q. *"My wife's birthday is coming up; maybe I'll try to pick out some maternity clothes. Thoughts? Concerns?"*

A. Plenty. Whatever you buy, keep the receipt. Better yet, don't even try. Stick to jewelry, gourmet chocolates, and whatever is on her list. Here are eight reasons why not to try:

1. "How big do you think I am?"

2. "They call it a muumuu because it makes you look like a cow."

3. "It's a little late now . . . I think I'm having contractions."

4. "Oh, this will be nice for the next time I feel like going out in public in maybe five years."

5. "This is tiny."

6. "This is huge."

7. "But Molly just gave me all her sister's maternity clothes."

8. "That's pretty! Who is it for?"

Lucky Guesses

Q. *"I walk into the office one morning, and a female co-worker takes one look at me and says, 'Is your wife pregnant?' I was so flabbergasted, there was no point in trying to lie—the truth was obvious."*

A. It is traditional not to tell anyone about a pregnancy until the first trimester is safely under your belt, so to speak, but women's intuition waits for no man. You simply weren't prepared. Every pregnant father should be aware that women's intuition is incredibly powerful, and also quite random. It could be your boss, it could be a co-worker, it could be a woman who hardly knows you at all, but at some time—maybe even before you're even sure that your wife is pregnant—they will ask. Be prepared, stay cool, and *lie*. Your wife is depending on you. Think about it: How are you going to explain that after two months of hiding it from all of your nearest and dearest, you went ahead and told Kerrie in accounts receivable?

The New Place

Q. *"I know there is a lot going on right now, but we're thinking that we should move out of our apartment into a real house. Any advice?"*

A. It is a cruel but logical fact that just around the time you are having your first baby is the same time that many couples feel the need to get into a bigger apartment, a bigger house, or, at the very least, out of your parents' place. The terrific thing is that "moving" actually ranks higher than "having a baby" in the charts of psychological stress inducers. Moving tends to be underrated, but our subconscious is deeply devoted to our familiar surrounding. Familiarity breeds a sense of security.

The other great thing is that, once you begin your move, since your pregnant wife is not supposed to lift heavy boxes, use harsh cleaners, or smell paint fumes, she will be left primarily on the sidelines where she can focus all her energy on telling you how to do things more efficiently or carefully or both.

Still, if you need more space, you need more space. Moving while the baby is neatly packed inside Mom is probably easier than moving while Baby is out and about. And it will be at least fifteen years before the baby can help move things, and even then he'll be all sullen about it. Anyway, last we checked, mortgage rates were at all-time lows, so go for it.

Vanishing-Twin Syndrome

Q. *"I have heard of something called vanishing-twin syndrome. Is that for real?"*

A. Okay. This one is kind of spooky. We now have better technology and thus an increased medical surveillance of early pregnancy. One of the discoveries that has been made because of this is that there are many more twins conceived than had previously been believed. However, early in the pregnancy, sometimes one of the twins just naturally stops developing and disappears. That part is completely factual. Now, the part about the baby who does survive having special psychic powers or a split personality or a dark second soul is all reckless conjecture.

CHAPTER FIVE

The Third Month

What Your Wife May Look Like

At the beginning of the third month, the fetus inside your wife is distinctively human, with a large head, small rump, and fully formed toes and fingers. Though your wife can't feel it, the fetus is now active. The fetus is kicking, clenching and unclenching its fists, pressing its lips together, frowning, and making other facial expressions—and so is your wife, as a matter of fact.

What Your Wife Will Be Complaining About

- Exhaustion
- You
- Excessive salivation (It's medically known as ptyalism, but don't let her try to say it. Ptoey? Surely it was given its name by the same medical humorists who decided "dyslexia" would be a fine name for people with letter issues.)
- Indigestion
- Indigestion tablets, which make her nauseated
- That she's still dying to tell everyone she's pregnant but is now convinced that people have guessed
- That nights are not as long as they used to be
- That not knowing the baby's gender makes it impossible to paint and furnish the nursery, or buy clothes, or lock down a name
- These "complaining about" lists, which are demeaning, sexist, and incomplete
- Morning sickness
- No morning sickness, so something must be wrong
- That aspirin and acetaminophen are good drugs, such nice, friendly, headache-curing drugs—how could they be bad for your baby?
- These maternity vitamin pills are so large she needs to eat them with a knife and fork
- That *American Baby* and *Parenting* magazines are still not as interesting as *Vogue* and *Elle*
- Or that *American Baby* and *Parenting* now hold her interest more than *Vogue* and *Elle*, and it scares her
- Emotional highs and lows, fear, ecstasy, anxiety, and elation, often all at the same time, and it scares her

A Couple of Things to Say to Let Her Know You're Caring, Sensitive, and Up On the Required Reading

1. "Isn't it great to know that right now the placenta is beginning to produce its own progesterone, taking over the function of the corpus luteum?"

2. "You know, the danger of Rh sensitization occurs only when an Rh-negative woman is pregnant with an Rh-positive child—and a simple dose of Rh immunoglobulin soon after delivery will prevent the dangerous antibodies from forming. Honey, are you asleep?"

What to Buy This Month

You've got a lot of basics in the closet already, so now you can feel free to purchase actual toys, but don't get behind on the necessities. Buy, buy, buy, and don't look back. Look, there is a chain of stores called buybuyBaby. What other product category could get away with such an unapologetically blatant sales pitch of a name? Spend Spend Women's Fashions? I don't think so. But when it comes to outfitting nurseries, the marketers know that you need to spend, you want to spend, you're going to spend. You just don't feel right until you know some purchase has been made that will meet Baby's every imaginable need.

ESTIMATED COSTS, MONTH THREE

Basics: $880
Basics plus extras: $2,595

Basics

Baby book

Bathtub seat

Blankie

Blocks

Cheap pillow for crib—wait, no! The latest word is that pillows are unsafe.

Bubble gum cigars that announce "It's a Boy" or "It's a Girl" (or even a few real cigars if you know anyone who would appreciate both the retro humor and the cigar itself)

Coloring books

Crib bumpers—wait, no! A few years ago these were indispensable and darling, but now, apparently, they are death traps, and you'd be a fool to use them.

Crib pad (under sheet)

Hair detangler comb
Knee pads for crawling
Musical pull toys
Raggedy Ann or Andy
Rubber ducky
Shampoo eye shield
Video camera
(Do not buy a jack-in-the-box—though
  classic, these traumatizing toys were
  invented in an earlier era when scar-
  ing the children was the goal.)

Extras
BB gun
Legos (not for the baby, for you, but
  justified as "an investment for the
  future")
Model train (same)
Tinkle Targets—floatable bull's-eyes
  for teaching little boys to aim
  (or make your own by sketching
  appropriate targets on toilet paper)
Video-editing software
Wide-angle lens for digital camera
10 TB external hard drive to store
  photographs and videos

Making Not Working Work

You really can earn thousands in your spare time, working from home! How? Just by considering all the money you are not spending on child care, commuting, and taxes as virtual "income." This is called creative accounting.

Early in pregnancy, many couples begin to wrestle with the big questions of how parenthood is going to change everything. One of the paramount questions is work. Together, it is time to sit down with a scratch pad or possibly an Excel chart or even an accountant and do the life math. The simple question: Can you afford for her to stay home? However, there are many factors to tabulate. It's not too hard to figure, but don't leave out all the details. It adds up. The following work sheet will help:

Gross salary, including bonus, commissions, and tips	+
Minus . . . federal income and social security taxes	−
State and city taxes	−
Cost of commuting	−
Cost of child care	−
Cost of takeout and restaurant meals because she's too tired to cook after a long day at work	−
Cost of excessive toys and fancy baby clothes purchased to assuage guilt over being away from Baby	−
Cost of stuff your first, dishonest nanny pilfered	−
Extra fees (and grumpiness) from day care when you show up late for pickup	−
Extra cost of pediatric visits for all the colds, flu infections, and odd ailments picked up at day care	−
Net income	=

Minus net income after computations above	–
Plus potential income from her part-time work at home selling overpriced beauty products to her friends (and/or whichever particular part-time scheme she is hatching)	+
Cost of flowers, gifts, and special dinners to make her feel like she's not "just a housewife."	–
Cost of new stroller because the other one is so crummy and now she goes to the park practically every day	–
Cost of replacing the window treatments that would never have bothered her if she had still been at the office all day	–
Total loss of real net income	=

A New Father's Spiritual Journey

Moving from the exciting early months into the grinding middle trimester is an ideal time for reflection. There is certainly no comparison between your experience of pregnancy and your wife's visceral, all-consuming experience. However, when it comes to contemplating the spiritual change that parenthood will bring, there is no reason you can't compete! In fact, with fewer physical aches and pains, you may be even better suited to really focus your energies on the psychic trauma and existential angst that can come with bringing a child into this world of woe and uncertainty.

Yes, you are at the dawn of a new era, and the awesome responsibility may lead you to ponder the deeper philosophical issues that have always faced man. What is the meaning of our lives? What role will religion and a relationship with God play in your life? After all, you had to go to Sunday school—your kids will have to go, too.

Go ahead, think, ponder, worry, explore, pray. You'll want to get your spiritual journey complete and done before the baby is actually born. Why? Because nature (or God, take your choice), as it so often does, has arranged things with beautiful, purposeful harmony. For just as the questions about life's meaning rise to a fever pitch, countervailing influences rise up to meet them. The answers to the great questions? Yes, but it is time to feed the baby, change a diaper, do an errand, or maybe just nod off because you were up half the night. The chaos of baby raising soon makes it impossible to contemplate our ephemeral nature, or the subtle ethical dilemmas life poses. The minute you start thinking philosophically, next thing you know, you wake up and there is drool on your shirtsleeve. (If you're lucky, it's your own.)

It has been said that the unexamined life is not worth living. And that is something that you will really have to give some thought to, but right now the Diaper Genie needs emptying, you haven't fixed that window latch, and the dentist called.

WHAT YOU MAY BE CONCERNED ABOUT

Varicose Veins

Q. *"I'll be honest. I think varicose veins are gross. I'd take stretch marks over them any day. Is there anything to do to prevent them?"*

A. To help your wife avoid varicose veins and other circulation disorders, put three-inch wood blocks under the foot end of your bed. A slightly tilted bed will help balance out the effects of daylong gravity.

An interesting side effect of the tilted bed is increased adnogginal circulation. All the blood rushes to your head, and you may have especially vivid dreams. If you have a severe case, you may have what is known scientifically as "tomato head." If this is the case, you probably have the bed at too steep an angle.

Any efforts on your part to make use of this slightly off-horizontal situation to add a touch of novelty to your evenings are attempted solely at your own risk. Especially if the wood blocks under the bed legs are not all that secure.

Boy or Girl?

Q. *"Everyone we meet seems to have a very definite idea whether we're having a boy or a girl, based on how my wife is carrying, or her complexion, or the alignment of Jupiter and Mars. The remarkable thing is that they all seem to be so sure. Is there any truth to all these old wives' tales?"*

A. Old wives can be a real problem. Take mine . . . please! Irrelevant kidding aside, almost everyone has an ultrasound or two nowadays, so if you want to know, just find out! But there are many other old-fashioned methods that don't involve covering your wife's belly with goop and scanning her with high-tech instruments. For those who would rather stick with some form of intuition, here are some of the more popular old wives' tales:

- The faster the heartbeat, the more likely it's a girl.
- Carrying high and long means a boy; low and wide means a girl.
- Easy pregnancies are boys; difficult ones, girls. No comment.
- If you put on a lot of weight where you sit, it's a girl. Really no comment.
- Food cravings mean boys; chocolate cravings mean girls.
- Italian old wives believe that if you go for the heel of a loaf of bread, it's a boy.
- A clear complexion means a girl; a poor complexion means a boy. (But girls will cause more headaches during their adolescence, so it all evens out.)
- Pump some stereophonic Motown into the womb. Girls "dance" to music; boys go to sleep. (This holds true up to and including junior high school.)
- Smooth hands mean a girl; rough hands mean a boy; dry, scaly hands mean you should be doing the dishes for your wife more often.
- When the mother gains weight, you're having a baby, but when Dad gains weight? He's having too many helpings. Wait, that's not a wives' tale, that's a wives' comment.
- A dream about trying to pick out a prettier postage stamp means it's a girl; a dream in which you really don't want to stop to ask for directions means it's a boy. Okay, yes, now I'm just making stuff up.

Her Food Cravings

Q. *"My wife still hasn't sent me out to get pickles and ice cream. Is something wrong?"*

A. She will. Some supposedly well-researched and ridiculously best-selling guides to pregnancy have stated that pickles and ice cream is just another old wives' tale. They could not be more wrong. Pickles and ice cream is an indisputable fact of modern-day pregnancy. Fathers shouldn't feel intimidated or uncomfortable about it. To help expectant fathers serve the very best pickles-and-ice-cream combinations to their wives, we offer some suggestions:

As a general rule, the saltier pickles are best with the deeper flavors: the various chocolates—Ultra-Fudge Chung, Heavenly Hash, Dark Chocolate Thunder—as well as pistachio, coffee, and cookie crunches. After all, the salty caramel and pretzel-infused ice creams that have become so popular are working in the same gustatory range.

For the exotics—curry pickles and *senfgurken*—we recommended one of the lighter sorbets. To complement the robust flavor of kosher dills, nothing is quite so perfect as peach ice cream.

Chowchow pickles, of course, are a natural with chocolate chip. Mint Oreo was positively made to be served up with baby gherkins. Finally, short-brine bread-and-butter pickles go best with a simple vanilla ice cream.

Q. *"We're hip urbanites, and this whole pickles-and-ice-cream concept seems very old-fashioned. Isn't there something more fashion-forward that my wife can crave?"*

A. While pickles and ice cream is classic, there are no limits to the foods a pregnant woman can suddenly demand at two A.M. A longtime vegetarian friend of ours suddenly had to have a ham sandwich late one evening. These *nouveaux* cravings can be just as pressing and twice as difficult to satisfy. Does your twenty-four–hour store carry pasta salad with sun-dried tomatoes? Marinated organic baby corn? Soy–carrot muffins? Find out *before* you start making foolish promises while you're pulling on your shoes and pants. There is no more lonely feeling than cruising the darkened storefronts knowing that if you don't come home with strawberry–rhubarb pie you might as well not come home at all.

Telling

Q. *"We've been dying to tell people that we're pregnant, but now that we can, we're not sure what the best way to go about it is."*

A. The end of the third month, when the odds of miscarriage drop significantly, is the traditional moment to tell the whole world, "We're pregnant!" But how? And whom? When to post? When to tweet?

Chances are, your wife has already told her best friend and her mother. (Do you get to pick a couple of trusted friends? No, *your* friends cannot be trusted.) If you haven't told the grandparents-to-be, they are surely first on your list, and not just because of familial proximity. It's good to start with people who will express nothing but unbridled joy and happiness. Unless your parents are still harboring severe doubts about your chosen mate, or severe misperceptions about their own age, grandkids are the best news they could hear.

The rest of the phone calls are up to you. The priorities are siblings, close friends, and people you bet that you would get pregnant first. When you start getting bored with "Guess what?" as an opening gambit, get creative. There are plenty of ways to break the news. "How many grandkids do you have . . . so far?" "I know something you don't know." "We did it!" has an interesting double entendre.

Whom to tell? The basic rule of thumb is that a person should have some sense of who you are before they are informed that you are expecting. But even here, you should decide what is right for you. If it seems important, then by all means let toll collectors, waitresses, and telemarketing representatives in on your joyous news.

As far as social networking goes, there is only one rule: Be sure that everyone who might conceivably expect a phone call gets one before you post the big news. Once it is out there, there is no telling quite how the information will diffuse. Try explaining to your best friend from college why she had to hear it first from her cousin Bill, who is in a fantasy baseball league with your husband's colleague's real estate lawyer.

One word of legitimate practical advice before you make your calls: The first natural question in response to your announcement is, "When are you due?" (Unless a more natural question is, "Are you going to get married?" or possibly, "Are you two out of your minds?") When people ask when you are due, add two weeks to the actual due date your doctor provided and tell everyone—even your nearest and dearest friends and relatives—*that* is your due date. Why lie? It is a strategic choice that will save you headaches later. During the final month, especially if you are actually late, you will both be going insane, thanks to people

saying, "Have you had it yet?" "When was your due date again?" and "Haven't you had that baby yet?" As if you hadn't noticed that your due date has come and gone. The phone calls from folks "just checking in" accelerate as the due date approaches. The subject line of every e-mail should be, "No, not yet." When you call home, the first words out of your mouth have to be, "No baby! Hi, Mom, it's me, just calling to . . ."

Why start all that any earlier than necessary? In any case, the date is just your doctor's educated guess, so you're not really lying, just adjusting.

Special Celebrity Feature!

Greetings, incredibly famous actor/singer! Thanks for having your assistant/personal manager pick up this copy of *What to Expect When Your Wife Is Expanding*. We feel confident that you and your equally famous wife are facing many of the same issues that the rest of us are, but, of course, there are special challenges to having a baby in the white-hot glare of publicity. Here are a few tips and pointers:

1. You'll want to get the "first photo" negotiations out of the way soon. No point dragging it out.

2. Your wife's early pregnancy will be referred to as a "bump." It may be

that noncelebrities can also use this nickname, but we've never seen it used outside of celebrity gossip magazines and TV.

3. Make sure your publicist and personal assistant attend childbirth classes along with you. They should be just as prepared as you are.

4. Get your applications under way because, for each birthed child, you'll want to adopt a couple of children of complementary but different skin colors.

5. Consider a bigger mansion.

6. Buy the movie and TV rights to this book! The heck with Cameron Diaz and her movie version of the original *What to Expect* book. What a fine and hilarious TV series or blockbuster summer movie this could be! I see Ryan Reynolds as the baffled first-time father, and Brad Pitt as the more experienced father of six and part-time humor book writer.

7. Tweet! This is especially vital for the first-time celebrity parent. Mix equal parts giddiness, profound sense of responsibility, and self-deprecating confusion. This will create the illusion that you're just a normal guy anyone can relate to. Don't try to be funny about your wife's pregnancy—believe me, I know how much trouble that can cause.

8. To conclusively demonstrate your commitment to fatherhood, cancel or rearrange a major project, or at least pretend to.

9. Appear on Nickelodeon's *Kids' Choice Awards*, or accept a gig as a voice-over in a kids' animated film. Being in projects with a kid audience demonstrates paternal yearnings nicely. Also, it will give you a head start for when your five-year-old wants to see what you do and all your films are R-rated.

10. Skip Cannes.

11. Stay away from the nanny! What are you doing with a nanny already, anyway? But when the time comes, we suggest you take the preventive measure of hiring an aging spinster who looks as much as possible like Mrs. Doubtfire. And still, stay away from her!

Celebrity Baby Name Guide

Hey, pregnant megastar! While we've got your attention, please note that the single greatest challenge that lies ahead is naming the baby. Unfortunately, you are obliged by the unwritten code of celebrity to step far outside the realm of ordinary names. Yes, the general public will make sport of your eccentricity, but all press is good press. How to choose the right name? First, eliminate the one hundred thousand most common names. Now, the best thing would be to consider words that have seldom been names before, like Apple or Scout. How about Kiwi, Spring, Mandible, or Doorstop? Another less exciting option is a place that hasn't been a common name yet: Tucson, Peoria, Hampshire, or perhaps Tampa-St. Pete? Finally, if you resist these ideas, you are permitted to choose square-to-be-cool retro names, as long as they are very, very square. Mildred, Prudence, or Hortense for girls; Stanley, Irving, or Horace for boys. Or perhaps even older than retro? This is an area that is bound to be explored soon: Beowulf, Balthazar, Tristram, Telemachus, or Cleopatra? By the way, why is the biblical name Noah so popular, while his sons, Japheth, Shem, and Ham, and grandsons Lud, Magog, and Ashur never get the nod? Food for thought!

CHAPTER SIX

The Fourth Month

What Your Wife May Look Like

The fourth month includes that wonderful moment in between the green morning sickness tones of early pregnancy and the pale, drawn complexion of late pregnancy—yes, the famous "healthy glow." Catch it if you can. Although this is the period when most people make their pregnancy public, your wife will still be dressing in the loose shirts and stretch pants known as basic denial wear. She's trying to achieve the "you're hardly showing" look.

Or . . . she could be of the "dying to show off my pregnancy" school. In that case, she may actually develop a swayback accentuating her small rounded belly. She will wear all-out maternity clothes, modeling each outfit for you, pulling the fabric back to ensure that the abdomen is not lost in the folds. (Don't point this out; just say pregnancy becomes her, or she's glowing, or something like that.)

What Your Wife Will Be Complaining About

- Exhaustion

- You

- That all the other women in the ob-gyn's waiting room are further along

- A decrease in urination frequency—a temporary reprieve

- That her breasts continue to enlarge, and it ain't over till it's over

- Leukorrhea (we don't want to talk about it)

- Increase in appetite for foods she can't have

- Swelling of the feet, ankles, and cell phone overage charges

- Parents and friends, who were too excited, not excited enough, or just didn't say the right things when she told them

- That now is no time for you to start taking hula hooping so seriously

- That you told people she wanted to tell first

- That books insist various strange syndromes are incredibly rare, when she's quite sure she has them

- Increased sexual desire or total loss of sexual appetite (no, you don't get to choose)

- The size of your home or apartment

- That she just realized there are recessive genes for red hair on both sides of the family and she isn't sure she will be able to bond fully with a red-haired baby

- That her regular clothes are uncomfortable, but she is still unwilling to commit to true pregnancy clothes

- That books promised, they *promised*, that morning sickness would end, but you're not being supportive because you don't think her case will hold up in court

- Emotional highs and lows, fear, ecstasy, anxiety, and elation, often all at the same time

A Couple of Things to Say to Let Her Know You're Caring, Sensitive, and Up On the Required Reading

1. "Did you know that right now our baby's sebaceous glands are producing sebum, which mixes with skin cells to form the vernix? Vernix! *Our* baby's vernix."

2. "Diuretics to stop water retention—though still prescribed by some doctors—have been shown to be useless and in fact harmful during pregnancy, causing nutritional deficiencies, fatigue, depression, insomnia, and damage to the kidneys. And *Dianetics*—don't even go there!"

3. "Oligohydramnios is the condition of having too little fluid in the amniotic sac, while polyhydramnios is the condition of having too much. Thank goodness you've got just-right-hydramnios!"

What to Buy This Month

With the passage of the first trimester, the risk of miscarriage is mostly past. Now it is time to forget about the little trinkets and start bringing home the big-ticket items.

ESTIMATED COSTS, MONTH FOUR
Basics: $1,672
Basics plus extras: $2,082

Basics
Baby-size shoehorn
Dora the Explorer licensed apparel
Changing table/dresser
Crayola crayons, in the 64-color box
Crazy straws
Crib
Crib mirror
Food grinder—little hand-cranked item that turns peas into thoroughly mashed peas in an instant
Glow-in-the-dark stars to stick on nursery ceiling
High chair
High chair cushion
Hip-sling baby carrier
Jug of Desitin
The Wiggles DVDs (yes, you have to—but BluRay is not necessary)
Snugli (rhymes with ugly, fittingly)
Spoons shaped like airplanes
Stroller

Extras

Baby Jogger, so Baby can have a smooth ride while you take a run, or you can hang it on the garage wall as a nifty device for gathering dust

Saint Bernard dog, with brandy dram, to come to your rescue

Your Social-Media Pregnancy and Birth

It has been said that, in general, women use Facebook to connect, and men use it to boost their egos. That sounds about right, although you could replace "Facebook" with "life" and you wouldn't be far off.

In any case, we live in a digitally connected world, which means you can instantly share every profound observation, political concern, emotional state, thought, worry, plan, surprise, blemish, coffee mishap, hangnail, and—wait! Before you log out, remember that your wife is also your "friend." And if you tweet, she no doubt follows. Whatever you express—or fail to express—will be duly noted. Now is not the time for reticence or decorum. Everyone loves a prospective dad bubbling over with unbridled excitement and pride, right? Or perhaps there is some middle ground, but tread it carefully. The Chinese ancients said it best: An unkind text falls easily from the Blackberry, and a thousand horses cannot drag it back. Like? Retweet?

Before you start the predad babbling, let's back up and take a broad look at the thorny issues that lie before us. We are all in the early arc of a vast new learning curve. We learn as children how to talk to family, friends, strangers, authority figures. We learn (after saying some of the darnedest things) what is appropriate. Posting your words into any of the available venues on the Internet means talking to anybody at any time. How do we address an audience that is both sitting at work and sitting in bed at night? They are colleagues and guys you knew in high school. They are cousins who agree with your politics, and ex-girlfriends who don't. They are ten years older and ten years younger than you. They love the same music as you and have never heard any of it. Now: Jot them a quick note to tell them you're expecting a baby.

The easiest strategy is the Big Blue Elevator. Life is just one long elevator ride. Keep it light. Keep it generic. Be aware that even people you don't know, who shouldn't really be listening, are with you, nodding politely. This is easy, but does limit you to a fairly superficial take on things. In fact, your updates can easily be cut and pasted from other sites. "Can't believe I'll be a dad in just five months. Excited!"

The next strategy is to create a sort of personal brand. Think about other people's perceptions of you. What are your special passions? Maybe you'd like to be the straight shooter: "Five months and eleven days to our due date." Sure, it may seem a little cold, but taken collectively, this sort of journalistic reporting can create the impression that your life is an important endeavor, and each crossroad is worth noting.

Most people recognize that their various connections are looking for entertainment, and the posts that get the most attention are generally comic. So post funny and post often! Still, there are all kinds of funny. Creating a specific brand of comedy and sticking to it will set up the right expectations, making it more likely that readers will pick up on what is intended as a joke, instead of misinterpreting your sarcasm or even just thinking there must be a bad typo. What's going to be your online persona? There are many choices.

The classic wry observational humorist. Think Seinfeld. "Can't believe I'll be a dad in five months. Suddenly it seems like everybody is pregnant, am I right? You turn around . . . hello! Another pregnant lady!"

Maybe you're the self-deprecating type. "Can't believe I'll be a dad in just five months . . . so not ready!"

Take it further and you can be the self-defeating nebbish. "Can't believe I'll be a dad in just five months . . . How long will it take for the baby to lose respect for me? I'm giving it a year."

Maybe you can even go right to the dark side and live there. "Can't believe I'll be a dad in just five months. If I am the dad."

Whatever the personality and tone you choose, just remember there are no take backs. To paraphrase your mother: If you can't think of anything nice to text, don't text at all. Or to paraphrase the brave rebel protesters: The whole world is watching . . . and just waiting for your next laughable blunder.

So how far apart are the Facebook posts? Every four minutes is too much. Every four months is too little. Playing Bejeweled Blitz when you just announced the baby is coming any minute is bad form. Friends and acquaintances are waiting for the news! They do not want a blow-by-blow account of anyone's labor, no matter how interesting it is to you. On the other hand, if you commit to a blog, your readers are there because inquiring minds want to know. Spill all. Quote your laboring wife. Include photos of the hospital food tray. Some stray thoughts about renting a TV, what sort of people become nurses, did you leave the stove on at home?

Public Displays of Affection

Q. *"Now that my wife is obviously showing, our pregnancy feels so public. I know it's probably ridiculous, but I keep thinking that people will know that we 'did it.'"*

A. Yes, that is ridiculous. Your feelings are silly and wrong. Nonetheless, if you are uncomfortable about this public display of your sexuality, one simple solution would be to tackle the issue head-on. If strangers nod and smile, tell them immediately that you only "did it" once, and it wasn't even that much fun. This straightforward approach will make everyone feel much more comfortable about you and your pregnancy. It will get rid of the proverbial "elephant in the room"—so to speak. Better yet, when you sense public disapproval, confront the people who are lifting eyebrows and explain quietly, calmly, and in simple but clear language how a man and a woman make a baby. This may not make everyone comfortable, but at least you will all know what happened. And it's good practice for later.

Am I a Sexist?

Q. *"Lately, my wife calls me a sexist more and more. I may not be a card-carrying member of the National Organization for Women, but I was never 'the enemy' before. Is it something about pregnancy that brings out this issue?"*

A. Indeed, pregnancy is a phenomenon so patently unfair to women that it often causes a rising stridency in their responses to any and all gender-related issues. However, avoiding the trap of being dubbed a sexist—and having no defense—is easy if you follow a few simple rules. Stick to the guidelines below, and you'll have plenty of ammunition the next time she calls you a soulless troglodyte.

- Try to cut down on your use of the expression "chickie baby."
- Watch an Oxygen reality show and pretend to like it.
- Use those Sacagawea and Susan B. Anthony dollars. They're handy once you get used to them.
- Stop arguing that figure skating and gymnastics are not really sports.
- Watch the NCAA Final Four in women's basketball, too.
- Actually read some of the articles in *Glamour* or *Elle* while you're scanning them for babes.
- The next time something needs to be fixed around the house, offer to fix

dinner while she does the repair. And pray she says no.

- Even if you mean it as a compliment, never bark at a woman.

Part of the issue may be that with the complicated task of parenting bearing down on you, so to speak, your wife may be anxious that your inveterate sexism will lead you to create unnecessary gender distinctions in your children. However, you'll find that politically correct gender neutrality is on the wane. It peaked somewhere back in the 1970s—possibly during the airing of Marlo Thomas's TV special *Free to Be, You and Me*. Essentially, the feminists won all the major battles, and the last few skirmishes have become less and less mainstream. Today, very few parents will deny that girls are genetically encoded to enjoy wearing tulle and tiaras, keep diaries, and love butterflies, and that even the smallest boys cannot resist flinging objects down stairs just to see how much noise they make. So if you're having a boy, you can feel free to decorate the nursery in blue, and buy clothes, bibs, and sippy cups with your football team's logo on them. If you're having a girl, you can decorate the nursery pink, scout local dance academies, and set aside a bathroom drawer for hair thingies. (If you want to decorate the nursery now, but you're not finding out the gender, green is nice.)

The Antidog Contingent

Q. *"It's so annoying when people ask us what we're going to do with the dog! As if no one ever had a dog and a baby in the same house."*

A. This is a common pet peeve (pun fully intended) of pregnant dog owners. Many strangers, even friends and family members, seem to believe that a baby and a dog cannot coexist. There is no shortage of snappy answers to the question, if you feel like it. "We're going to put her down" will get jaws to drop. "A muzzle and whip work wonders." Or you could explain the elaborate system of putting an "invisible fence" belt on the baby to train the dog by giving it a mild shock anytime it gets too close.

Or you could be more patient and explain that issues with pets and babies are extreme rarities. You know your pet as well as anyone. A sensible, conservative introduction and keeping a watchful eye on the interactions is generally all that is needed. Your listeners will nod politely and think that you are misguided and possibly criminally negligent, but hey, you tried.

Being Concerned About Everything

Q. *"What I may be concerned about? What am I NOT concerned about? Our drinking water? My 401k? The local public school? That creep two doors down? That weird mold in the basement? . . ."*

A. The dawning sense of responsibility and anxiety about parenting can sometimes lead to more generalized anxiety. You may find yourself worrying about seemingly minor things. We can't address every unfounded fear, but here are some FAQs (fathers' angst-provoking questionings) and the simple solutions that should put your mind at ease:

The baby won't look like you, or will look like you, depending on your self-esteem.	**Easy Answer!** All babies are beautiful . . . to new parents.
You're not sure you can function without a full night's sleep.	**Easy Answer!** You're not doing all that great with a full night's sleep.
What if your wife is suddenly having the baby and you can't get to the hospital?	**Easy Answer!** That's what reading all these books is all about. No problem. You've studied and prepared and memorized, and you are now totally ready to coach your wife, catch the baby, and await medical assistance. Or maybe you should go back and read that section one more time.
The national debt is spiraling out of control.	**Easy Answer!** Having that first baby just cut your family's per capita share of the debt a full 33 percent!
You're going bald.	**Easy Answer!** Neither your wife—nor any other woman—cares anymore.
Medical insurance costs are crippling!	**Easy Answer!** The family plan covers as many kids as you care to have. So having more kids is essentially saving you money!

You don't feel particularly wise and fatherly.	**Easy Answer!** No one does. Luckily, there is a wonderful resource that will allow you to handle any situation, to offer guidance that is upright and sensible, to offer advice that is both moral and accessible as well as logical and achievable, to set limits, and to offer just the right sort of unconditional love . . . TV sitcoms. Choose your own favorites, but if in doubt, go way back. *Leave It to Beaver, The Brady Bunch, Full House,* Cliff Huxtable of *The Cosby Show, Everybody Loves Raymond.* Each offers its own special blend of well-meaning fatherliness.
You'll never be able to save enough for college!	**Easy Answer!** No one else can, either.
How are you ever going to get the band back together?	**Easy Answer!** The "parents who rock" subculture is alive and well. If anything, the guys will be more anxious than ever to carve out a weekly rehearsal night. You just might need to add more soundproofing to the basement ceiling.
Your wife won't let you call the boy Mike, Junior.	**Easy Answer!** Your wife is right. Back to the drawing board. Come up with a new name, not just your own name again. Among other things, statistics show that "juniors" as a whole have more incidents of mental instability and low self-esteem. It is easy, facing a wee infant, to underestimate the impact of being called Little Mike, or Mikey (as a grown man). Relations between father and son are complex enough without labeling him "mini me."
The Sun is a dying star.	**Easy Answer!** Yes, but there are about nine billion years left. If you regularly set aside just 1 percent of your paycheck, and put it in a conservative index-based mutual fund and leave it there for one million years, you actually will have enough money to pay for your children's college education and then some (barring inflation or catastrophic asteroid collisions).

The Ring

Q. *"My wife has removed her wedding band. I don't know exactly what she's planning, but I like it here. Should I ask her about it, or just wait until I find my stuff outside the front door?"*

A. Relax. Your wife is undoubtedly taking a simple precautionary measure to avoid discomfort when edema (swelling) affects her hands. Shoes, belts, watchbands—everything must be adjusted. In the old days, doctors prescribed a low-salt diet to prevent this water retention—but we now know that some salt is necessary. A pregnant woman's increased blood capacity simply requires a bit of stretching all around. Of course, it is also perfectly normal to experience no swelling, so it may be that your presumptions aren't so far off. It may be that your wife has cashed in the jewelry in preparation for the day she hits the road and leaves you crying in your beer. Has she bought a motorcycle lately?

Toys!

Q. *"We found out that we're having a boy. Can I start buying race car sets?"*

A. This may not have occurred to you yet, but one of the best side benefits of having children is that you will soon be able to buy toys "for the kids." In fact, it seems quite possible that the slight (unspoken!) preference that fathers have for male progeny derives more or less directly from their preference for rockets, planes, and crossbows over stuffed animals, puppets, and dollhouses.

Below is a list of some highlights to get you started. Some people might advise you to not wave them all in at once or to try to stay somewhere in the realm of what is age appropriate for your child. The heck with that. No matter when you start buying these toys, it will be completely transparent to your wife that you are buying them for yourself. Furthermore, there is a fair chance that, during the pregnancy, she will find your toy-buying sprees "cute" or even a demonstration of your enthusiasm for becoming a parent. Later, during those sleep-deprived early days, she may be less open-minded.

Dear Santa,

I have been a very good man this year, and I am having a baby, so please bring me:

A Serious Kite. Not just your basic diamond with a tail, although that would do in a pinch. Box kites, biplanes, pirate ships; there is no end to the available designs.

Slot-Car Race Track. Figure eight is a good start, but what about that one? Yeah, the big box.

Night-Vision Goggles. Cool, right? Turns your living room into a video game. Oh, and they even might have a practical use: finding things without turning on the light and disturbing the baby.

Zip-Line. Two trees, a winch to stretch wire, and no fear. Good luck selling this one.

Microscope. No, not the science lab kind you bend over to look at premade slides of dragonfly wings. The one you want has a scanner that hooks up to a television monitor and feels like an electron microscope.

Remote-Control Helicopter with On-Board Video Camera. Twenty years ago, a high-tech toy was slapping some glow-in-the-dark paint on a yo-yo. Now you can shoot high-definition video of your living room from a whirling six-inch-long minicopter. What will another twenty years bring? I'm betting on cloaks of invisibility.

Q. Faking Couvade

"My wife is now convinced that since I haven't experienced any symptoms of Couvade syndrome—sympathetic pregnancy—that I'm not sympathetic to her plight. Should I fake it?"

A. You may have to. (After all, she probably has been faking it now and then to spare your feelings.) Once her mind is made up, there will be no point in quoting statistics about the rarity of the syndrome. You'll have to complain about your swollen feet, absentmindedly rub your belly, drink milk, and pretend to throw up every morning. But there are two other approaches you may want to try first.

The first approach was developed by Dr. Rickard Grolsch in his ongoing Princeton Institute studies on male response theory. His advice is to point out to her that from a psychological viewpoint most Couvade victims are not "sympathetic" but jealous. "Sympathetic pregnancy" is a misnomer, and gives too much credit to men who are selfishly trying to co-opt the pregnancy for themselves. You are a well-balanced, appropriately empathetic person—a helpmate and friend—who understands that the burden of pregnancy, along with its joys, will always be the woman's, first and foremost.

If that doesn't work, you may want to try a more general response strategy developed by a team of Northwestern University relational psychologists led by Dr. Wilma Krobb. They recommend that, rather than directly attacking any tender issue, the husband simply make an absurd statement and then defend it vociferously. You might recall that we suggested just such a ploy earlier with "the cat said it" defense to a foot-in-mouth moment. This is a much more advanced system than Grolsch's, though it is, of course, based on his groundbreaking treatise, *Changing the Subject*.

Krobb et al recommend you begin by speculating that the guppies in the fish tank seem to be depressed. The researchers note that the key to success in this strategy is to insist that this is not a casual joke but an icy reality. It may seem at first to increase your wife's ire, but if you persist, she will eventually forget what she was complaining about. Other possible themes: "A stranger has been in the house," "I suddenly put the pieces together and realized my old college roommate isn't who he says he was," "I keep smelling things from the past."

The worst case is that you will actually induce a psychotic episode and will need professional help to escape the personal demons you have unleashed. Actually, that is a pretty bad worst case, isn't it? Well, sometimes drastic measures are called for when you *really* don't want to start a tiff with the wife.

CHAPTER SEVEN

The Fifth or Sixth Month— Somewhere Around There

and

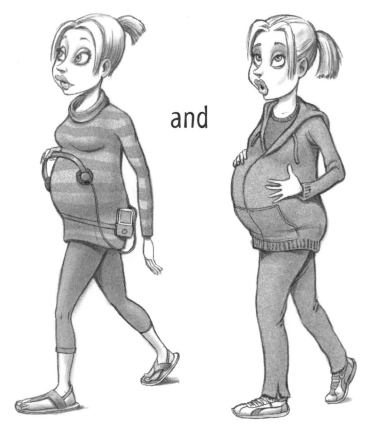

What Your Wife May Look Like

The belly can be denied no longer, and with it comes True Maternity Wear from such haute couture labels as La Stork, Dressing for Two, and Preggers of London. Seemingly, overnight facial expression and general complexion have gone from "the joy of pregnancy" to "I've been pregnant forever."

What Your Wife
Will Still Be Complaining About

Exhaustion

You

Absentmindedness

Fetal movement, not enough or too much

Breast changes: heaviness, fullness, tenderness, tingling, darkening of the areola

Your interest in the above

Absentmindedness (Oh, yeah, she already complained about that.)

Backaches, side aches, leg aches, fingernail aches

That the eleven o'clock news is too scary

That food cravings are your body's way of telling you what nutrients it needs, so there must be something vitally necessary in chocolate

Mild edema, or a swelling, of the feet, and "mild" is all it takes to make all her shoes, except the ratty slippers, painful to wear

That Baby's hiccups have stopped being cute

People stealing the name she wanted to use, making it impossible to use it because every other baby has it, and the whole point was she didn't want a trendy name

That she has finished reading everything the Internet has to offer on pregnancy and now needs new sources of anxiety

A recurrent need to feel her tummy

That friends and acquaintances need to feel her tummy

Emotional highs and lows, fear, ecstasy, anxiety, and elation, often all at the same time

A Couple of Things to Say to Let Her Know You're Caring, Sensitive, and Up On the Required Reading

1. "Your complexion looks fine, Honey, but, if you're worried about it, you might want to try a vitamin B_6 supplement of 25 to 50 milligrams, which can help alleviate hormone-related skin blemishes."

2. "Stanislavsky's acting techniques—which involve awareness of the different sets of muscles in the body—can be applied to preparation for childbirth. Perhaps you could have an improvisational birth?"

3. "Did you know why you're not supposed to lie down flat on your back? It's because that position can put too much pressure on your inferior vena cava. No . . . I'm not saying your vena cava is inferior! In fact, I'm sure it's above average."

What To Buy This Month, Whatever Month It Is

In the rush to buy all the stuff at the toy and baby-furniture stores, you've probably overlooked all the little basics you'll need from the local pharmacy. Stock up now, and save on errands later.

ESTIMATED COSTS, THE MIDDLE MONTHS
Basics: $419
Basics plus extras: $529

Basics
Alphabet and number refrigerator
  magnets
Backpack carrier
Baby bath
Baby lotion
Baby oil
Baby powder
Baby shampoo
Baby toothbrush
Bassinet (no, it's not a musical
  instrument; ask your wife)
Humidifier
Mechanical swing
Playpen
Portable crib
Walker

Extras
Personalized child-size pool cue
Safety scissors (great for craft projects
  later; great for your clumsy
  pregnant wife now)

Sex During Pregnancy

Q. *"My wife has been, well, sexually hungry just when I'm feeling kind of ambivalent about this odd new body of hers. I've heard this is not unusual, but I don't want to make love that much. Plus, I worry about hurting the baby."*

A. Fear of hurting the baby is a very good "sensitive male" response to your wife's constant sexual demands, but it's far from the only excuse at your disposal. Try: anxiety about burgeoning paternal responsibilities, headache from fine print in pregnancy guidebooks, a pulled muscle from constructing the crib, or the "thought we could quit after it worked" argument. If the pressure does not relent, your last, cruel resort is to hint at the unattractiveness of the beached-whale look. Don't take this step without first thinking long and hard about whether you can deal with the repercussions. Remember, you might someday want to do it again.

Diapers and Landfills

Q. *"I've heard that diapers are an environmental disaster, and I'm not quite sure how they are causing the polar ice caps to melt, but in any case, is there anything I can do to be more responsible?"*

A. When the first edition of this book was published in 1993, there was still an active debate between those who swore by disposables and those who believed that cloth diapers were the environmentally conscientious choice. When the second edition was written, it seemed the diaper debate was all but over. Today, thanks to growing environmental consciousness, the cloth option is back!

While the vast majority of new parents go straight to the big boxes of disposables, there are those who demand the more natural material. There are still cloth diapers, diaper services, and pinless Velcro diaper covers, yours to be purchased if you feel that only natural cotton is good enough for your baby's bum. For more information and some righteous information, you'll find plenty of outposts on the Web of the militant procloth junta. In fact, there are legitimate arguments on both sides. Users of traditional cloth diapers almost all employ a "diaper service" to clean and supply these all-cotton nappies. So the trucking, chemical cleansing, and production of cloth diapers somewhat undermined the efforts to be "green." Even if you wash your own, you'll be using a lot of extremely hot water and detergent. But your baby will be doing their thing in cotton nappies. The cloth-diaper folks also point out that babies might potty train earlier because they are more uncomfortable and aware of when their diapers are wet. Seems like an argument that cuts both ways.

There is a growing middle ground in the diapering field, as entrepreneurs are trying to create the next big system, with washable cloth liners, improved "used" diaper storage, even washable reusable wipes. Take a look around the Internet. Another compromise measure, if you like the convenience of disposable but want to stay as natural as possible, is to find the companies that sell versions of the disposal diaper that use fewer chemicals and less plastic. According to reports, they work just about as well, with the only downsides being that they cost a bit more and, for most people, have to be ordered online and shipped. You could probably do almost as much good for the environment by skipping a few changes. After all, the "real" disposables can absorb six gallons of liquid, and if you don't believe it, let a kid wade into the lake in one.

All that said, for most parents, you might as well suggest they telegram the grandparents or hire a wet nurse. They love their disposables. Better Living through Chemistry! They'll tell you it is the only sensible choice unless you live in a geodesic dome four hundred miles from the nearest outpost of civilization. Most of the articles in parenting and baby magazines and major Web sites agree. On the other hand, are those magazines and Web sites likely to go out on a limb and claim that cloth diapers are better—or even a legitimate option—when the bulk of their advertising comes from Pampers, Huggies, and the rest?

Or you could potty train at nine months like our hunter–gatherer ancestors did. Apparently, the trick is just to carry the kid around with you all the time naked. There is actually a growing movement (speaking of . . .) of people who encourage parents to begin toilet training that early, and that is the idea in essence. You just watch the baby for the telltale facial expressions. Eventually, you'll learn to spot the signs that the baby is about to go and be able to get them onto the potty. Sounds more like parent training than potty training, but if you've got the time, go for it. No one ever regretted that they didn't change more diapers.

The author has actually had personal experience with both traditional cloth and disposable. They were both okay. The kids were equally blasé about toddling around the house with a full load. But the biggest factor in moving from cloth to disposable was a short conversation I had with our local diaper service. (We join the conversation in progress):

AUTHOR: But we returned all seventy diapers, and you only dropped off fifty.

SERVICE: If your standing order is for seventy, then a hundred and forty diapers are in circulation.

AUTHOR: Yes, but I promise you we aren't hoarding diapers. We need seventy to get through the week.

SERVICE: Are you double diapering?

AUTHOR: Uh, yes, at night.

SERVICE: Make sure to separate them when you put them in the pail.

AUTHOR: Separate them?

SERVICE: When they spread out the diapers to be counted on the conveyor through the electric eye, the people who separate them sometimes miss some if they're stuck together.

AUTHOR: Oh.

SERVICE: Is there anything else we can help you with? Sir? Hello?

AUTHOR: Oh . . . uh, good-bye.

SERVICE: Bye.

Yes, there are people somewhere who go in to work every Monday morning and take their place at a mechanical conveyor line where they separate dirty diapers for an electric eye. Did Mike Rowe ever take that on in *Dirty Jobs*? Think about it the next time you see your wife squinch up her nose and call out, "It's your turn." And if choosing disposables means that there is going to be another former diaper separator looking for a new job, I can't help but feel it's ultimately a good thing.

Becoming a Father

Q. *"Just being pregnant has meant so many changes in our lifestyle, our planning, our relationship. The prospect of fatherhood is beginning to terrify me."*

A. Having a child will mean changes, no doubt about it. Along with the great joy and satisfaction that the baby will bring into your home come limitations, sacrifices, and worries. The best advice we can offer is to prepare by tapering off. You don't want to go cold turkey. Adjusting now to just a few of the deprivations to come will make the initial shock of fatherhood that much easier. Here are ten simple ways to get ready:

1. Stop seeing movies in the theater. Young parents see movies only at home, so if you don't stop going out to the movies now, there will be an awkward lag of six to eight months during which every new release is a movie you've already seen. Netflix

can help. On the other hand, many couples simply lose the attention span or the two relatively uninterrupted hours necessary for movies, anyway. Try sitcoms.

2. Explore additional takeout options. You'll want more choices than pizza and Chinese when you're eating it every single night of the week.

3. Check out the very late-night television schedule. Sadly, much of basic cable is swamped with paid programming of dubious quality. So, unless you're interested in getting involved in buying real estate or breakthrough kitchen products, you might want to invest in a DVR, or some of those extra sports packages like MLB Extra Innings. With a few favorite shows on queue, you might actually look forward to those two A.M. feedings.

4. If your wife can't get to sleep, drive her around the block seventeen times and then carry her back into the house.

5. Go to the drugstore and say loudly, and without shame, "Excuse me, where are the wipes?" And while you're at it, you might as well buy a few now. For a very different challenge, go into a local biker bar and say loudly, "Excuse me, where are the wipes?"

6. If you smoke, try doing it secretly in the garage. Do it barefoot, too. The cold cement adds to the effect. Don't put it out with your foot, though, and don't forget to pick up the butts *and* the spent matches.

7. Slice a heated hot dog into ten sections, then cut each circle into choke-proof quarters, and allow to cool and dry out for one hour. Then eat the whole platter yourself because the kid wasn't interested. Use a small rubberized spoon to add to the challenge.

8. Practice holding your breath for two minutes and seventeen seconds. (The amount of time a skilled parent takes to handle a particularly foul diaper change—we old hands call it a "six-wipe" change.)

9. Buy yourself clothes that are too small, then pack them in boxes, carefully label them, store them, and forget about them forever. It may seem pointless, but so are bathrobes for one-year-olds, and we own two.

10. Carry a ten-pound sack of sugar everywhere you go to build upper-body strength.

Things That, It Turns Out, Are Not Funny

Q. *"I keep telling her that I was just kidding."*

A. Husbands need to be increasingly aware that there is a fine line between the affectionate "you're an idiot" and the despairing and resentful "you're an idiot." It is, of course, impossible for us to foresee every possible misstep and immaturity, but here are ten things that, it turns out, are not funny.

1. Extralong sideburns

2. Hiding the last piece of ice cream cake

3. "Pull my finger."

4. Your new golf shorts

5. Insisting that a layette means a little lay

6. That viral video of wedding cake mishaps (your comic is her tragic)

7. This book (sexist, demeaning, silly, and not at all useful)

8. Demonstrating how you can flip a pancake by flicking the pan instead of using a spatula (successful or not)

9. Teaching your toddler snappy catchphrases (i.e., "Show me the money," or "That's what she said!")

10. While she's sleeping soundly, drawing a window frame with a baby looking out—on her belly

Taking the Pledge

Q. *"I'm trying to support my wife by joining her in giving up smoking, drinking, and coffee, but it's driving me crazy."*

A. It's great to be supportive, and your wife will find your temperance admirable. She will feel that you are working as a team, and also she won't have to face temptation from your cigarettes, martinis, or triple-shot cappuccinos. If you can do it, Godspeed, O Perfect Husband!

We recommend another approach. Since she can't drink or smoke, and may be cutting back on caffeine, you should think of yourself as smoking for two and drinking for two. If your wife can eat for the baby and for herself, surely you can order a double and drink a toast to your better half!

And by the way, here's the good news: The day your wife found out she was pregnant, she became your designated driver for the next year, even longer if she's breast-feeding. It's a handy thing, too, because you could use a drink.

Perineal Massage

Q. *"We've heard that perineal massage can help better prepare for childbirth."*

A. Perineal massage. Sounds dirty? If it doesn't, it should. Because it is. Oh, you can volunteer to learn the proper techniques, consult with your own doctors, discuss how some practitioners believe it can help avoid episiotomies, treat it as clinically and professionally as you like . . . it is still inescapably in the realm of naughty bits. That may be a good thing or it may not. In either case, just make sure you are both on the same page, of the same manual.

Staying Married

Q. *"We both wanted to have this baby, but now that we're pregnant, we just can't seem to get along. She's so moody and unpredictable."*

A. You're not the only person who has to adjust emotionally to having a baby—this period of transition can be hard on your wife, too. And don't forget, she's got all the minor physical discomforts of pregnancy to deal with, as well. So be patient, understanding, forgiving, thoughtful. Listen to all her complaints and criticisms without being petulant or defensive. Give, give, give. Buy flowers, write poems, and stay home from work, just to take care of her. How can you do it? How can you manage to transform so completely? Simple: by matching every thoughtful act with a passive-aggressive jab. A long, low whistle when she steps on the scale ("It was just a joke, sweetie") or cooking heavily spiced stews, chili, thick pungent soups—there are a hundred little ways to needle your mate, and after a long day of feeling put-upon, coming up with them will be second nature.

A second option is to take the offensive. Start complaining about your day the minute you hit the front door, don't even pause for breath for ten to fifteen minutes, and then say, "Oh, Baby, I'm sorry. Going on and on about my troubles. How are you feeling?" She'll either buy it or slug you.

The final remedy is to provide your wife with other outlets for letting off steam. Is she talking to her mother often enough? Does she have plenty of other pregnant friends? Do whatever you can to foster these relationships. The more they hear, the less you have to hear. You do run the risk of magnifying her annoyance, if, for example, her new girlfriend is married to some saintly do-gooder of a husband. Generally, you'll be better off if you can encourage her to vent to women of a previous generation. Mom and aunts were in relationships and marriages with men who were, relatively speaking, Neanderthal in both practical and emotional ways. After all, if you can't measure up to Uncle Stan in the sensitivity department, there's nothing we can say to help.

CHAPTER EIGHT

The Seventh Month

What Your Wife May Look Like

That healthy white glow is now here to stay, and she is too tired to make any sort of facial expression at all. Yes, her breasts are now larger. No, you can't touch them—they're painfully sensitive. She will also stop denying the need to get off her feet, to the point of asking old ladies and war veterans to give up their seats for her.

What Your Wife Will Constantly Be Complaining About

- Exhaustion

- You

- Clumsiness, disorientation, headache—a bit like being drunk without the increase in tranquility and loss of inhibition

- Shortness of breath, dizziness, heartburn, nasal congestion—like smoking without getting to light up

- Strong and frequent fetal movement—now that the novelty has worn off

- That she's tired of complaining about the same old symptoms and wants new symptoms

- Itchy abdomen

- High cost (and limited use) of maternity panty hose

- Sciatic nerve problems, which are both painful and difficult to pronounce

- Her company's maternity leave policy

- That your company has never even heard of paternity leave

- That her best friend's ob-gyn sounds nicer than hers

- Her weight

- That you haven't even had the baby yet, and there's a product recall of one of the things you bought

- That you picked now, when she is as big as a house, to go on a little diet and lose ten pounds

- That people make jokes when she enters an elevator

- That medical textbooks (purchased for complete, scientific details of every single possible problem) are expensive, and their prose style is tedious

- Nonalcoholic beer, which just doesn't do it

- The realization that Baby won't arrive in time to be a deduction for the current tax year

- That she doesn't want to know what sex the baby is, but it seems unfair that the doctors know

- That you are halfway through this silly humor book and you still haven't read a single page of the real pregnancy books

- Emotional highs and lows, fear, ecstasy, anxiety, and elation, often all at the same time

A Couple of Things to Say to Let Her Know You're Caring, Sensitive, and Up On the Required Reading

1. "You know they say that vitamin E can be very helpful in preventing varicose veins; of course, I mean vitamin E in the form of d-alpha tocopherol acetane. Mixed tocopherols don't have any effect on varicose veins, naturally."

2. "You can practice the breathing techniques you learn in class by trying to control the pain of a headache or a stubbed toe. Every little accident is an opportunity."

What to Buy This Month

By now, many pregnant couples will know their baby's gender and so can begin reinforcing sexual stereotypes right from day one by choosing boy or girl clothes, boy or girl colors for the nursery, and boy or girl careers toward which to pressure.

ESTIMATED COSTS, MONTH SEVEN
Basics: $722
Basics plus extras: $2,490, plus $24.95 per month

Basics
Lullabies (CDs or downloads)
Rearview-mirror enhancer, so you can see the back seat
Baby monitors
Baby sweater with fruit motif; or baby sweater with truck motif
Bathtub (infant size, not regular)
Child-size bathroom sink (fits in tub)
Infant-size party dress or baseball uniform
Juice dispenser
Night-light
Nursery art
Piggy bank
Rocking chair
Supply of disposable diapers—a couple of crates to get started
Teeny-tiny baby fingernail clippers
Travel diaper kit

Extras
All the premium cable TV channels (parents never go out)
Christening gown (if you're Christens)
Dr. Seuss, complete
Tiara or football helmet
Second Tivo (I'm telling you, parents really never go out)

TRICK QUESTIONS

Your hubby senses are tingling! Danger lurks: new ideas; potential threats to your space, schedule, automobile, or self-esteem. Here are just a few seemingly innocent questions. Can you foresee the issue? A quick, thoughtless answer can send you spinning into an abyss of recriminations! Test yourself today by imagining your wife has just asked you one of the questions below. Remain ever vigilant!

Do you think we need a shed?

Did you see that redheaded woman?

Would you like my mother to come for dinner?

You didn't forget, did you?

Do you ever look at my Facebook wall?

What does "private browsing" on Safari mean?

Do you think my friend _____ is attractive?

How wide is the den?

How long have you had that (goatee/moustache/beard/earring)?

And because she is pregnant and worried and feeling guilty about everything, learn how to answer this special series of questions. (Hint: The answer is always "No.")

Do you think it is bad that I . . .

ate a Pringle?

had a caffeinated soda?

used my old hair conditioner with that bad chemical in it?

stood near the microwave?

gained a pound?

had my cell phone near my belly?

accidentally swallowed a bug?

have polarized sunglasses?

used the "bad" sunblock?

swallowed a bug on purpose?

worry so much?

Let's Be Alarmist

Q *"Reassurance, reassurance, reassurance. My wife and I are sick of all the books and doctors and friends comforting us and telling us that there's nothing much to worry about. We want to worry."*

A Most people would like to go through all nine months of pregnancy thinking happy thoughts, but let's face it, you're not really pregnant if you're not going crazy worrying about all the things that could go wrong, feeling guilty about all the little things you may have done wrong, and poring over every new pregnancy and childbirth article in the newspapers and magazines. Paranoia is a perfectly healthy reaction to pregnancy.

We have already promised that this book would not raise unreasonable fears, so we feel honor bound not to tell you that your tap water may already be limiting your child's intellectual potential; nor will we tell you which brands of coffee use beans sprayed with dangerous pesticides, or that too much tofu and soy product is really bad for you. It would also be wrong for us even to bring up such unlikely disorders as Flanders' syndrome, fetopelvic blastula rentinculitis, or even gestational aneuristic halitosis. Their incidences are so statistically improbable that they are hardly worth mentioning.

Have we piqued your curiosity? That's why the Internet was invented. You are just a high-speed connection away from a virtually unlimited collection of half-truths, misinformation, opinionated speculation, and fringe medical theories. Search for "pregnancies gone awry," "babies gone crazy," "obstetricians gone wild," or "the dangers of sunblock or dying your hair." It's all there. Just steer clear of the well-traveled, professionally designed sites like WhatToExpect, BabyCenter, Parents, WebMD, or Parenting. What's the fun in getting carefully edited pregnancy and medical information? The crackpots, herbal medicaters, and antiestablishment reactionaries are much more interesting.

If you still find that your need for anxiety is outstripping the available Web sites on pregnancy, you might want to start searching for blogs and rants about the sorry state of America's educational system, the effect of television on modern culture, the political history of the Middle East, or the fragility of the ecosphere. And that's just for starters. It's the new Internet "six degrees of separation" rule. If there is something out there that a single person is worried about, you can still find it within six links.

Sex During Pregnancy

Q. *"What exactly are the chances of having sex during pregnancy?"*

A. Sexual relations during this physically and emotionally traumatic period are nothing to worry about. You should remember that the statistical chances of having sex during pregnancy are very low, almost negligible. Odds are you'll never have to deal with it. Still, every pregnant father worries about it, and yes, it could happen to you. If your thirty-week-pregnant wife is feeling amorous, don't panic. Yes, she can be an intimidating physical presence, but if you proceed with caution, and don't bring any unrealistic expectation to the process, you may find that you actually enjoy it.

Doing the Lamaze

Q. *"Do I really have to take Lamaze classes? Can't I just read a pamphlet for a few tips and just be really pleasant and positive during labor?"*

A. To start with, what were once widely known as Lamaze classes are seldom actually called "Lamaze" anymore. They tend to go by more innocent and generic names like Childbirth Preparation or Birthing Readiness. The Lamaze organization seems to have taken a hard-line all-natural approach, and most hospitals don't go for politicizing the process. There was always something a little cultlike about going to a Lamaze class. And who was this Lamaze, anyway? Now, it just doesn't matter. But you still have to learn to breathe funny and watch a scary movie or two. Watching every episode of *Sixteen and Pregnant* or any other pregnancy reality show is not sufficient preparation. Sorry.

In any case, don't let the prospect of a little tedium and having to hear the words *labia* and *nipple* spoken aloud in public keep you away from class. This is your one chance to do something useful! You're the coach, man, and whether your personal style is more Rex Ryan or Herm Edwards or Bill Belichick, this is an opportunity to get involved.

Use the classes to get yourself into a childbirthin' frame of mind. The game is tied and going into the ninth inning. It's overtime, gut-check time, and you had better know what all your options are. What will you do if the obstetrician notices a breech condition and calls an audible for a cesarean? What if your wife is clearly tiring, but the anesthesiologist says it's too late for an epidural? If you're going to coach this birth, you better have a game plan, and class is the place to get it.

The classes themselves vary greatly from instructor to instructor. The better instructors show a lot of films, go over breathing and relaxation techniques every week, talk a lot about pain, and otherwise provide down-and-dirty preparation. The worst classes start at the very beginning, like a sort of remedial health class. You'll get the charts of the fallopian tubes, the egg and the sperm, even mitosis and meiosis if you're really unlucky. Then, they walk you through fetal development, and get to the breathing gimmicks and "Choices in Pain Relief" only in the last meeting or two. The sole advantage of this type of class is that it's slightly more likely to give you a small suitable-for-framing diploma in childbirth.

Putting Together the Crib

Q. *"I'm having a little trouble putting together the crib. Any advice?"*

A. This important ritual is one of the very few preparatory events that is exclusively in the male province. It is to be taken seriously. Do not ask for advice. Do not ask for help. Find some quiet alone time to read the instructions over before you begin.

After you build the core physical structure, and place the mattress, of course, your wife will reassert control. There are many options and choices for bedding. At minimum, to go with a warm comforter and lighter blankets (seasonal) you'll want thick cotton sheets, with a sheet guard on top in case of leaks. The mattress pad (natural fiber

preferred) goes under, with an under-mattress pad liner, and because of the danger of bedbugs, the mattress itself should be in a sealed bedbug-resistant bag. With all these in place, you may find that you can actually forego the mattress itself.

Home Alone

Q. *"My wife is considering a home birth. But I don't know, I guess I'm more traditional."*

A. What are you talking about? You're not more traditional, you're more sane. Home birth?! Yeesh! All right, pregnancy isn't a disease, and modern hospital care may be a little dehumanizing and expensive, and sky-rocketing malpractice awards make doctors too quick to resort to a C-section. Sure, sure, sure, but those are not reasons to just give up and stay home. Obviously, the hospital has better backup for medical emergencies, but that's just part of it. Do you want to listen to your answering machine picking up right in the middle of active labor? Does your bed at home adjust to seventy-five different positions? Is your television mounted to the ceiling?

Nonetheless, home birth is on the rise. Proponents of home birth extol the psychological benefits of familiar surroundings. Some people have reported that they chose it to save money. Surely, there are few better arguments for continued and better health-care reform.

Go to the hospital; you'll love it. In fact, more often than not, once she has gotten comfortable, your wife won't want to leave the twenty-four-hour nurse attendants, the adjustable bed with handy swivel tray, and the free, professional babysitting. Only those icky meals and pushy inquiries from the insurance company will finally urge her out and on her way.

Pregnancy Simulations

Q. *"My wife says I'm a jerk. While that seems to me to be a rather broad, overgeneralized statement, she has suggested that I go to one of these pregnancy-simulation weekends."*

A. It may not be the cure for jerkiness, but a well-managed, professionally run pregnancy-simulation weekend can change your attitude about what your wife is going through. The specifics vary, but generally these camps and spas attempt to approximate the experience of late pregnancy. With cute names like "The Nine-Month Weekend," "A Little Bit Pregnant," and "Daddy's Turn," they offer a variety of programs, but they follow the same pattern. Naturally, it begins when you strap on a forty- to seventy-pound water-filled "womb." (Your womb is heavier than

your wife's because it is in proportion to your body weight—no breaks, mister.) You then ingest some mild drugs, which will make you feel disoriented, experience strange dreams, experience mood swings, and want to pee every half hour. While the staff smoke and drink in front of you, you'll enjoy a smorgasbord of fresh vegetables, whole wheat, bran, iron- and calcium-rich foods, and, of course, pitchers of milk. Finally, you will be asked to pass a greased honeydew melon. No, not really.

Rubber Baby Buggy Bumpers

Q. *"Some acquaintances seem to think that the wife's belly is fair game—they reach over and rub without even asking!"*

A. As the due date approaches, you will find that—much like rubbing Buddha's belly—it seems to be considered good luck to lay hands on that taut kettledrum that your wife is lugging around. The standard etiquette books offer little advice when it comes to patting other people's bellies. Is it acceptable among relatives? Close friends? Female acquaintances only? In a business setting? While pregnant women will have varying tolerance for the intrusion, most observers agree that by the eighth month, all pregnant bellies are awfully tempting targets.

The one group of would-be belly rubbers that must be turned down definitively are the ones who ask you, not your wife, for permission, as though you are the proprietor of a traveling freak show. It may seem difficult to turn down a polite request, but it really isn't. No explanation or diplomacy is necessary. All you need to do is feign complete horror at the suggestion. Furrow your brow and let your mouth drop open, as though they had asked permission to feel your armpit. You could even counter with "No, but I'm concerned I may have a hernia—would you mind having a check?"

If, on the other hand, your wife is *not* shy about sharing her overgrown personal space and positively wants people to feel the baby kicking, then you might as well charge a couple of bucks. You could probably bump it to five or ten when the baby is kicking. It may seem mercenary, but formula ain't free.

Breast Is Best

"My wife is on the fence about breast-feeding. She's heard all the health arguments, but she can't get used to the idea of it and is concerned about her figure, etc. What about me? Which is best, from a husband's perspective?"

Public-health advocates are increasingly pressing the importance of breast-feeding over formula. For some women, this additional pressure is just one more way they feel pushed around. As usual, our advice is to be "opinion neutral" for as long as possible. As soon as you become an advocate for one side or the other, you become an easy target.

That said, there are pros and cons. Breast-feeding definitely changes breasts, during the period of breast-feeding, from recreational to functional. But they'll be back. Breast-feeding is cheaper. Breast-feeding is healthier. Do you get the impression that we favor breast-feeding? You are right, and the fact of the matter is that all fathers should favor it. Why? Laziness, my friend. Laziness. When there are no bottles to be sterilized, dried, mixed, and given—well, there's really hardly any reason for *you* to even wake up.

P.S. If she does choose to breast-feed, just remember that, at some point, when Baby is six months old or so, you just go and grab away his favorite toy and stick it in your mouth. When he starts to cry, just say: "See? How do you like it?" It's important to let him know who is boss.

The Minivan (What You Are Really, to Be Honest, Most Concerned About)

Q *"Really? Really?! Do I have to go to the minivan already? It's just one kid."*

A Having your first baby is probably the biggest transition and transformation of your life. It will change your focus, your responsibilities, your day-to-day activities, and quite likely your car.

Don't panic! Keep your emotions under control and under wraps. No matter how impractical, if you play your cards right, you can keep your ride. Maybe you're still driving a gas-guzzling muscle car, maybe a temperamental but ferocious two-seat sports car, maybe a Hemi V8-powered extended-cab truck with hy-droformed frame and 800 foot-pounds of torque,* or maybe it's just old Bessie, the well-maintained but aging wheels that have been with you since high school. Don't let go! Never give up! As an about-to-be family man, you will eventually succumb to the irresistible practicality of the minivan, the bigger the better. But the baby-centric vehicle should be an addition, not a replacement. Just keep stacking up cars in your driveway. After all, how much can you get in trade-in for your self-esteem? Nothing.

Build more driveway if you need to. Expand the garage. Or just buy a full-body cover, which will make it appear that you are caring for some collectible gem, even if it is a ten-year-old Taurus with some serious transmission issues and no brakes to speak of.

*Actually, if you're driving a truck anything like this description, you certainly don't need any advice from me on maintaining your macho self-esteem. I'm sure you have no intention of trading in for a mom car. You may move on to the next section of the book. Sir.

CHAPTER NINE

The Eighth Month

What Your Wife May Look Like

The eighth month is when the slight waddle appears, especially toward the end of the month. By now, she will have gained twenty-five to forty-five pounds, and yet, from the neck up, ironically has the drawn face of a half-starved model. Most of her fashion choices are now made on the basis of how easy they are to deal with when she needs to pee every twenty minutes.

What Your Wife Will Be Complaining About

- Exhaustion
- You
- How much room you take up in the bed
- Her weight
- Bleeding gums
- That low-sodium food is low-tasty
- Unattractive distortion of her belly button
- Strong, uncomfortable fetal movements (new nickname for Fetus: The Karate Kid)
- The distance between the TV and the bathroom
- Braxton-Hicks contractions— if that was one, she doesn't want anything to do with real contractions
- That a month is a very long time
- The politics of taking hand-me-downs that you think will be nice and somehow turning down ones you think won't be
- That you never raise your hand in childbirth class
- Waistbands of maternity pants where it is unclear whether they go over the belly or under
- Extremely vivid and terrifying dreams
- That the numerologist says the due date isn't good
- That you just don't understand
- That somehow NetFlix makes you feel guilty about not watching enough TV
- That Hanna Andersson stuff is so much cuter but so much more expensive than Old Navy
- That she really misses sushi
- That you refuse to follow the advice of that other guidebook and call the local authorities to see if they will come by and check your microwave for leakage
- Nicknames you have given her lately (Moby, Barge, Her Hugeness)
- Disorientation and inability to focus—she now consistently loses to you at Boggle
- Emotional highs and lows, fear, ecstasy, anxiety, and elation, often all at the same time

A Couple of Things to Say to Let Her Know You're Caring, Sensitive, and Up On the Required Reading

Remember, unlike much of the information in this book, these are actual facts discovered in the actual reading of other books.

1. "Fetoscopy—which is less common than ultrasound or amniocentesis—allows doctors to photograph the fetus. But it is still primarily experimental, so we don't have to worry about it."

2. "When the baby has the hiccups, it may be because he is actually practicing breathing in the amniotic fluid."

3. "The breathing techniques taught in childbirth classes are found in other cultures. The Zulu, for example, teach pregnant women to go to the door of their hut each morning and breathe through each nostril, alternately."

What to Buy This Month

Don't panic! So maybe you're out of money—but you can't be out of credit yet. And if you are, start hitting up the grandparents-to-be. After all, they wanted this child as much as anyone.

ESTIMATED COSTS, MONTH EIGHT
Basics: $275
Basics plus extras: $410

Basics
Baby thermometer, and, yes, you
  want to splurge on the high-tech
  forehead scan because you'll be
  surprised how often the baby has a
  fever or you think she might have
  a fever or you think you might
  have a fever

Baseball glove
Diaper pail
Frozen dinners
Hooded baby towel
Juice canteen
Nasal aspirator
Teddy bear
Swaddling
Supply of baby Tylenol
Velcro diaper covers
Washcloths

Extras
Catcher's mitt/first baseman's glove
Clothing with team logos
Clothing with the insignia of the
  university you expect your child to
  strive to get into (especially bibs)

Clothing with family crest

Wipe warmer, which electronically warms diaper wipes for easy changes

Sex During Pregnancy

Q. *"My wife is so big, but she's so happy not to be using birth control that we're having more sex than ever. Are there any limitations we should be aware of in late pregnancy?"*

A. Good for you. Next time, write to *Penthouse*, maybe they'll care. Okay, fine, what was the question again? Oh, yes, limitations. As far as strictures go, unless your doctor indicates otherwise, a healthy pregnancy should cause no limitations, so long as you are both comfortable, with the only exception being that it is important not to blow air into your wife's vagina during oral sex. If this limitation creates a major problem for you, then you know something we don't.

By the way, if you happen to be reading your wife's copy of Vicki Iovine's *The Girlfriends' Guide to Pregnancy* (a popular read that's fairly humane in its treatment of husbands), you may come across the "at the hospital" example, regarding how soon after childbirth some couples start getting frisky again. (No, not intercourse—that's flat out.) What-

ever you do, don't point it out to your wife. She saw it, and, like every other woman in the world, she understood the story's underlying message: Some women are out of their minds.

Fetal Anger

Q. *"My wife has had a lot of discomfort with the baby kicking up a storm. In fact, I'm trying to convince her that he doesn't have a grudge against her. That isn't possible, is it?"*

A. Fetal distress is one thing; fetal emotional distress is another. The first is a physiological problem; the second is a psychological problem—in the mother. Unless you're a strong believer in original sin, or suffer from extreme paranoia (which is not unusual at this stage of pregnancy), it is reasonable to assume the baby holds no grudges. He's not mad at his mother; he's just getting crowded, feeling pressured, and finally kicking back. The same basic process will happen again during adolescence.

Photographing the Belly

Q. *"My wife has decided that she would like some beautiful and tasteful photographs of her maternity. But she is too self-conscious to go to a professional photographer, so I'm elected. Help!"*

A. We know exactly what she has in mind. Gauzy, artistic, dimly lit, seminude (but not revealing anything, you know) photographs of her cradling her belly or strategically covering her breasts. This endeavor will require fine aesthetic judgment, extreme tact, and a good eye for composition; and no matter how hard you try, you are almost sure to fail. Nonetheless, here are some tips that may give you a fighting chance:

- Don't try to use the camera on your phone; this will take a real camera.
- Avoid that distended belly button. I know, hard to avoid, but come at it from discreet angles, the sides, not head on.
- Use soft lighting. Better to see too little than too much.
- Do not use flash. Same reasoning.
- Use those sheets/blankets. Partial coverage will help frame the relevant elements.
- The right attitude is half the battle. Don't appear to be working too hard or sweating too much. No matter what she thinks of the photographs, you think they are beautiful.

The Baby Book

Q. *"We want to make a nice baby book, but everything we've seen is just too adorable for words. What should we do?"*

A. It is handy to have a book that lays it all out for you—from "Your impressions of Baby's first moments," "First birthday party," "First words," all the way to "Baby's first act of crummy teenage rebellion." But such books limit your creativity. Scrapbooking is now one of America's most popular hobbies, as well as one of America's newest verbs. Why not make your own? You should decide for yourself what's important, and in any case, you probably won't get beyond about the second month before the book just becomes a convenient holder for keepsakes that you're going to glue in and annotate "one of these days."

You could admit defeat from the start and, instead of buying a book, buy a handsome keepsake box and just throw everything into it. Another option is to keep a few stray notes and wait until the kid is old enough to put it together without your help. It's their book, after all.

You can probably think of all the basic keepsakes, significant moments, and plenty more, but here are some additional suggestions of things you might have missed:

- ID bracelet from the hospital (have you checked it, by the way?)
- Pressed flower from bouquet sent to Mom
- Pressed belly button stump
- Hospital bill (start in on the guilt from day one)

- Newspaper clippings from the day Baby was born: headlines, baseball standings, movie listings, horoscope, weather report, lottery numbers, real estate listings, and oh, that *Marmaduke*
- Memory of first time Baby was dropped on head and screamed so much it scared the hell out of you
- Lock of hair from first bad haircut
- Phone bill from first time Baby hit speed dial on cell phone and called your brother in St. Louis
- Photo of first time Baby allowed a hat to stay on for more than two seconds
- Memory of first time Baby found television sitcoms predictable (look for this one, generally, at around eighteen months)
- Souvenir shard from the first piece of antique crystal Baby destroyed
- Video of first time a hypnotist convinced Baby to act like a chicken

And why not leave room to encapsulate Baby's whole childhood? After all, she's still your baby until she leaves home.

- Baby's first f-bomb
- When Baby called you a hypocrite, accurately, for the first time
- Baby's first juvenile offense
- When Baby first went to Web sites Baby shouldn't have been on
- First time Baby spaced out and forgot to go to college interview

- First time Baby "celebrated" St. Patrick's Day and you got a phone call to come pick him up

You get the idea . . .

The Least Complete Baby Name Guide

James for a boy, and Emma for a girl. There, done. You don't even have to read the rest of this section.

Not good enough, huh? Well, it is true that naming your child is an extremely personal, idiosyncratic process. No two couples go about it the same way. Actually, there were two couples who went about it the same way, but it turned out that each father treasured a broken gold medallion, each was adopted, each married a woman named Helen, and each believed that Steely Dan was an underrated band; but that's another story, and a very long one, too. You just want to name your baby.

Naming the baby is an interesting and creative task, but it can be a sincerely awe-inspiring task, too. Naming implies possession, total responsibility. It is the first time that you must see your baby not as a mere miracle of nature, but as a budding participant in society. A name gives a child reality, definition, future. The implications are enormous. Names can be traditional—and stereotypical. They can be poetic—and strange.

They can bespeak glamour or simplicity, strength or wisdom, multiculturalism or rabid fundamentalism—all in a tiny being who has nothing but a few reflexes, a gnarly fresh belly button, and 20/400 vision. And you thought naming your cat was hard. What to do?

Play it safe and stick to our list. Sure, no one will tell you, "Oh, that's a beautiful name!" but that's okay, because when they do say that, what they're really thinking is, "Why do bad names happen to cute babies?" Here are five good names for each sex that may be a little dull, but that's what names should be: safe and innocuous.

Don't waste your cash on some fifty thousand–name paperback—this is plenty to choose from.

BOYS: Ryan, Joshua, Cole, Chase, Brian

GIRLS: Madison, Michelle, Sophia, Alexandra, Vanessa

Of course, we know that you won't take our advice. Days and weeks will be expended in the effort to come up with a name that A) you both like, B) isn't already in the top-fifty lists—or top ten, for that matter, and C) sounds reasonable with your last name. Perhaps the reason that naming has become such a traumatic ordeal is that it is the perfect, ultimately inconsequential decision to take your mind off all the actual worries surrounding having a baby.

While it is important to create a Web site for your baby as soon as possible, do not let the availability of a domain name influence your choice of their actual name! Do you really want your child named Ethan1168 Jones? Or Elizzzzabeth? Or Chris2pher? Let him pick his own screen name when the time comes. Anyway, screen names may seem important now, but the speed of technological advance means it would be foolish to predict what will be important in twenty years. By then, identities may be done entirely by iris recognition of video images.

Bonus Baby Namer's Tip: No matter how thankful your wife is, don't let her name the baby Epidural, or even Epi. If she really feels the need to thank the pain reliever, perhaps the name of your anesthesiologist would be a better choice. Best of all, wait a few days. You may find that her extreme appreciation will pass.

WHAT TO NAME YOUR BABY WHEN YOU'RE NOT SERIOUS ABOUT NAMING YOUR BABY

It has now been established through genetic mapping that one of the traits linked to the male sex is obsessive joking when faced with the task of naming a baby. Even before the physiological research, field observation had clearly supported the theory. According to 1990 figures, the average pregnant woman finds 3.5 joke names amusing and will laugh politely at roughly 7.7 names; a pregnant father, however, will laugh at up to 78.5 ridiculous names that he himself has made up. The disparity is a problem. However, the solution is simple. Men should simply realize that joking about names is to be saved for office and poker-night banter. Women should understand that the urge to make stupid suggestions is almost irresistible. For example, the list below has no real practical purpose except that, as a typical man, the author couldn't resist.

BOYS	GIRLS
Blind Lemon	Bertrude
Dagbert	Duchess
Enos	Tallulah
Fonz	Eccentricia
Fudgie	February
George Foreman VI	Jersey
Itchy	Kermette
Sluggo	Moxie
Pogo	Mylar
The Truth	Petunia
Upchuck	Pip
Walmart	Spaldeen
Zebulon	Corvette
Dacron	Taffeta
Shemp	San Diego
Bladd	Falala
Gillette	Glo-o-o-o-o-oria

SPECIAL REVISED EDITION BABY-NAMING NOTES

By the way, when this list was first published in the original edition, the name Mercedes was included as a humorous girl's name. Our apologies to the thousands of Americans who disagreed, because Mercedes has actually climbed onto the top one hundred American baby names for girls. While we found it absurd in 1992, because it seemed so obviously an automobile and not a person, apparently lots of other parents disagree. Porsche and Ferrari will probably soon make their way onto the real list, so in the meantime we've replaced Mercedes with Corvette. Joke or harbinger? We shall see.

In a related matter, shortly after the original edition of this book was published in the early 1990s, publishers in Europe decided to do translations, one in Dutch and another in French. Though delighted by the global attention, we were honestly a bit concerned as to whether the distinctly American cultural references would export. Is Ben & Jerry's a religion among pregnant Dutch women, as it is here? Do French men understand the difficulty of throwing away your childhood baseball cards? Not to mention that the very "expecting" pun upon which this tome rests is, apparently, not translatable.

Nonetheless, the book was duly translated, and *Een Baby Op Komst!*, and

Un Bébé Arrive were published. As an author and monolinguist (no, that's not dirty) with only a smattering of high school French, I nonetheless thoroughly enjoy flipping through both editions. My favorite translated article to ponder is the list of "names to avoid."

Apparently, in Holland, they agree that most of the original suggestions are poor choices (though they spell Fonz with an *s*—Fons), but they have replaced the girls' name Duchess with Hertogin, and replaced the boys' names The Truth and Upchuck with De Warrheid and Kotsje. Perhaps these are simply literal translations? If so, we remain concerned that perhaps something may have been lost in the translation.

Not so in La Belle France! In this edition, the translator has provided an entirely revised list. Apparently, in France, it would be *irrésistiblement drôles* to name a *garçon* Dagobert, Jean-Noël, or Donald. For the *filles*, you should resist the temptation to choose such names as Lolo, Rika, Ghislaine, or Bernarde. Oddly enough, Paulette, Julienne, and Liane also make the list—and they sound like fine names to this American. So be warned, if you plan on taking little Paulette to Paris, the waiters won't only be snobby—thanks to some obscure Gallic reference, they may just giggle at your baby!

Restless Leg Syndrome

Q. *"My wife read about restless leg syndrome. I actually thought that was an SNL parody, but I guess it's for real."*

A. During the last trimester, as many as 20 percent of expectant mothers may experience restless leg syndrome, an annoying sensation that is accompanied by an irresistible urge to move their legs. Still, that is only a very small percentage compared with the number of expectant mothers complaining of restless lug syndrome, the annoying sensation that your oaf of a husband should be doing something useful, accompanied by an irresistible urge to get him off his butt and at it.

It's Just a Dream

Q. *"Lately, my wife's dreams have become especially vivid. But when she tells them to me, I am still incredibly bored. Is there something wrong with me?"*

A. Not at all. During the last trimester, a woman's dreams become wilder, and will seem frighteningly real to her. Natural anxieties, increased blood circulation, hormonal changes, and sleep deprivation account for this; nonetheless, there is nothing more tedious than hearing a dream recounted. "Say, that reminds me of a story that has no particular beginning or end and doesn't make any sense.

Care to hear it?" Oh, sure honey, just let me know when a character is no longer who they started out as, or when you completely change where you are, okay?

And if you're thinking that you could try to interpret her dreams symbolically, forget it. First, the chances are good that your effort will make her cry. Second, these dreams are so bizarre that they defy conventional interpretation. Seasoned Freudian analysts have been known to hear the dreams of women in the third trimester and say nothing but, "Whoa, that's weird!"

If she or you would still like to have a go at interpretation, use the following basic guide:

What to Dream When You're Dreaming

The dreams of pregnant women can become incredibly vivid, sometimes frighteningly so. It can be reassuring to understand where these dreams come from, and who better than the husband to play psychologist?

As you form your analyses, realize that dreams cannot be understood merely as a group of symbols with standardized interpretations. The imagery of dreams has specific, personal meanings that defy simple attempts to classify and demarcate. On the other hand, dreams cannot be understood much at all, so you might as well try our glossary.

Here is your basic dictionary of dream symbols specific to pregnancy. Remember, our interpretations apply only to your wife's dreams. Any attempt to analyze your own dreams according to this chart could lead to hysterical pregnancy. And you don't want one of those.

SYMBOL/MEANING

BLUE, COLOR
Issues of cognition, or logic, or possibly that it's a boy

MOUNTAINS
Distant goal, separation

CARS
Wish to escape, or wish to move quickly, or wish that you could fit behind your own steering wheel

OLD WOMAN
Eternal female wisdom; or, to the contrary, fear that your mother-in-law will come to visit

CROSSING A RIVER
A change in attitude

PARALLEL PARKING
Resentment of having to "back and fill" or even execute difficult "K-turns" to exit from dining rooms of certain local restaurants

DESERT
Dessert

STORK
Diaper delivery service

DIAPERS
Fear of changing diapers

TEST, NOT BEING PREPARED FOR
Fear of labor

EATING
Generalized wish fulfillment

TREES
Hammock envy, probably connected to a strong wish to lie down

FLOATING
Fear that you now resemble a hot-air balloon

UNDERWEAR, GOING TO SCHOOL IN YOUR
Fear of same

FLYING
Fear, specifically, that you now resemble the Sea World blimp

WHALES
Childbirth class

CHAPTER TEN

The Ninth Month

What Your Wife May Look Like

Throughout the final month, your wife will generally give up on any effort to preserve her dignity. She will adopt the full-scale unapologetic waddle, go with minimalist hair care, and finally don the jungle-print muumuu (moo!) she swore she'd never wear. She alternates between wide-eyed hysteria and zombielike stupor, and takes off her shoes whenever she darn well pleases.

What Your Wife
Will Be Complaining About

- Exhaustion
- You
- All men
- That if it's false labor, it shouldn't be real pain
- Your weight
- Everything on the "What Your Wife Will Be Complaining About" lists for months one through eight
- That she needs an assistant to read the bathroom scale
- That the bathtub is not deep enough anymore
- That even maternity wear is no longer comfortable; she's down to exactly one dress that can reasonably be said to "fit," and she bought that at a drapery store
- Braxton-Hicks contractions
- That your double bed should be a queen; or the queen should be a king; or the king should really be a quarter-acre of firm mattress
- That the color you painted the nursery now seems too dark
- Mr. Braxton Hicks, his children, and his children's children
- That when you try to bring her breakfast in bed, the bed table—well, it doesn't quite work anymore
- Not getting a seat on the bus or subway
- Not being able to get up from her seat on the bus or subway
- The design ethos of your home as the nesting/redecorating instinct kicks in
- The automobile seat belt, which is now impossible to wear
- The color you repainted the nursery, which is too light
- People who tell her stories of very difficult births
- People who tell her stories of very easy births
- People who tell her stories
- That Baby doesn't seem to know that the due date has passed
- Fear of in-laws sending baby clothes she will hate
- That you really shouldn't be painting inside the house so much because the fumes can't be good for the baby
- Emotional highs and lows, fear, ecstasy, anxiety, and elation, often all at the same time

A Couple of Things to Say to Let Her Know You're Caring, Sensitive, and Up On the Required Reading

1. "While Leboyer childbirth seems appealing, there is no firm scientific evidence to support the arguments made in the book *Birth Without Violence.*"

2. "A nonstress test may seem like a pregnancy oxymoron, but it is called that to distinguish it from a stress test, which is essentially the same monitoring of the baby, with the added 'stress' being an oxytocin drip to set off contractions."

What to Buy This Month

The baby's got to eat, right? This is the month to get ready for the bottle or the breast.

ESTIMATED COSTS, MONTH NINE
Basics: bottle $759, breast $310
Basics plus extras: bottle $1,959, breast $1,510

Basics
BOTTLE-FEEDING
Automobile bottle warmer (plugs into cigarette lighter)
Bottle brush for cleaning
Bottle drying rack
Bottle sterilizing pan
Bottles
Formula
Hypoallergenic formula (just in case)
Rubber nipples

BREAST-FEEDING
Book on why breast-feeding is best
Breast pump
Nipple shield
Nursing bras
Nursing pads
Flowers, chocolate, jewelry, anything that will make your wife feel more appreciated and less practical

BOTH METHODS
Birth announcements
Car seat, up to 25 pounds
Car seat, 25 to 40 pounds

Extras
Library of works on child rearing and education: Jean Piaget, Maria Montessori, Jerome Bruner, *Marvin* comic strip compilations
Professional-quality baby scale—why wait for appointments with the

pediatrician to see how much Baby is gaining? DVD collections to indulge your own childhood nostalgia: *Sesame Street Old School, You Can't Do That on Television*, or Nickelodeon shows like *The Adventures of Pete & Pete* and *Clarissa Explains It All*.

What to Take to the Hospital

Her bag is filled with extra socks, bed-clothes, hairbrush, and everything else, but don't forget that you're probably going to be stuck in the hospital for a while yourself. Pack your bag now. Here are some recommendations:

- *A pillow:* for nodding off in chairs
- *A pack of cards:* for tossing into a hat from ten paces until your wife tells you to cut it out
- *Toothbrush, comb, fresh shirt:* but not a razor, for the unshaven look that is *de rigueur* for new papas
- Address book that includes phone numbers of all major relatives, or your cell phone that you double-checked is fully loaded with same
- *A tennis ball:* for giving excellent lower-back massage, especially during back labor, and also for bouncing mindlessly off a wall until your wife tells you to cut it out
- *A small harmonica:* Did you know that you can teach yourself to play a

few simple tunes in just minutes?

- *A handful of quarters:* in case of problems with the room phone (also good for tossing to see how close you can land them to the wall until your wife tells you to cut it out)
- *This book:* In those final hours, it's important to have a handy, reassuring reference work that includes everything you need to know about labor and delivery, so find one and take it along, too. This book, opened to pages 72 and 73, makes a handy eyeshade for catnaps.
- *Food:* She's chosen some nuts and dried fruit, but you need more than that to keep up your energy. Be sure to include the three basic food groups: fruits and vegetables (popcorn, ketchup, grape Kool-Aid); meats and fish (Slim Jims, pork rinds, Goldfish); cheese and dairy (Wheaties, Doritos, Tostitos, Pringles). Pop-Tarts also travel well, and fruit-filled Pop-Tarts encompass two essential food groups.
- *Music:* She'll ask for something soothing, but don't guess; ask about each choice *before* hitting PLAY.
- *Three stopwatches:* one for timing contractions, one as an emergency backup, and one for timing how long you can hold your breath until your wife tells you to cut it out
- *Pencil and pen:* for recording important thoughts, instructions, and things to do, and also for tossing up at the

acoustic ceiling in an attempt to make them stick, until your wife says she'll throttle you with her bare hands, contraction or no contraction, if you come up with one more stupid stunt

• *An expensive, beautiful, and incredibly thoughtful gift for your wife:* always a good idea during times of high stress

By the way, you do know we were kidding about the harmonica, right?

WHAT YOU MAY BE CONCERNED ABOUT

The Due Date

Q *"The doctors don't seem all that sure of the due date. Is there any simple way of judging how far along we are?"*

A In fact, there is. Much as timing contractions can tell you how far along labor has progressed, timing your wife's trips to the bathroom can give an excellent estimate of your due date. When she needs to urinate every hour, you can be sure labor is at least a month away. When visits occur every half-hour, she has about two weeks to go. Finally, when she is so completely exhausted from getting up constantly that she asks if you'd mind if she wet the bed, you can zip up the hospital bag and call work, because the long wait is nearly over.

By the way, don't tell her she can, because she just might, and you'll both regret it in the long run.

Pregnancy Brain

Q *"Is forgetfulness and general mental flightiness during pregnancy a medical reality?"*

A Apparently, the research is ambivalent. There is some evidence of an increasing inability to focus, and some diminution of short-term memory. These symptoms may be simply a result of exhaustion, not anything biochemical connected to pregnancy specifically. In any case, the scientific community is clear on one thing: Even if your wife is operating at 75 percent of her capability, she will still remember twice as much as you.

The Nesting Instinct

Q *"All of a sudden, my wife is up and about and changing where the furniture goes, suggesting new rugs, and cleaning like never before. Does this mean the baby is almost here?"*

A There are two exciting elements to watching the nesting instinct kick in. One is that this can be a sign of impending early labor. The other is that the house is impeccable! Most nesting behaviors are perfectly normal and no cause for concern, unless you find her outside actually gathering and weaving twigs together. Of course, the hyper-cleaning and organizing can be a shock. Here are some possible behaviors:

- Alphabetizing the soups
- Vacuuming the ceiling
- Cleaning the soap dish . . . using a different cleaning product than the soap residue itself
- Rotating the mattress, weekly
- Repointing the bricks
- Polishing your high school tennis trophies (which are plastic . . . and were being stored, in a box, in the basement)
- Recycling newspapers before you've read them

Crib Notes from Childbirth Class

Q. *"I missed a lot of our birthing readiness classes. What do I absolutely need to know?"*

A. Childbirth courses are like high school drivers' education courses. They're not strenuous, it's better to sit in the back, and the one thing not to miss is the films. Also, your wife may need to back and fill a couple of times or do a K-turn in order to get into her seat.

A father's preparation for childbirth should be focused on one basic goal: not fainting at the sight of your newborn. The films of childbirth, though lacking in compelling dialogue, have a solid dramatic structure and will teach you one simple lesson: the greenish, slimy, blood-streaked thing hanging upside down in the doctor's hands is, in fact, a perfectly healthy baby. No matter how prepared you think you are, you will think that something is definitely terribly wrong. The films aren't pretty, but keep your eyes open, because the real thing is no prettier. By the way, you may also want to avoid fainting when you watch the epidural needle go in, or even when they draw a little blood from your wife early on. You're light-headed, nervous, tired. It's perfectly understandable. Fine! I did almost faint a few times! There, I said it. Anyway, the last thing the nurses want to deal with is catching weak-kneed hubbies, so if you feel it coming on, head for a chair ASAP. There. One lesson done.

Aside from the films, of course, you'll want to learn a few breathing techniques and the information about all the available painkilling options so that you'll know how to explain to your wife why "you're not doing anything to help!" And don't get too riled up. You're something less than a nurse's assistant but more than an innocent bystander. The nurse and doctor will tell you what to do when the time comes.

Advanced Paternal Age

Q. *"I'm old enough that not only am I middle-aged, but I'm not worried about saying that I'm middle-aged. But here I am, becoming a new father. Are there any special issues older dads face?"*

There are both advantages and disadvantages to the midlife baby. For one thing, the chances that the baby will look like you are greatly enhanced. He, too, will be pudgy-faced, mostly bald, and convey a world-weary lack of expressiveness.

The middle-aged dad will definitely find interrupted sleep and the general alteration of lifestyle more of a shock. You've had that many more years of relative autonomy. On the other hand, you're that much further from those reckless, hard-partying days. A certain base level of maturity is a great thing to bring to being a father.

You'll want to pace yourself. Sheer physical tasks like gently jostling a baby around in your arms while walking in circles around the living room can wear anyone out. Later, you'll have to be careful about throwing out your arm trying to show off skipping stones, or throwing out your back trying to fold a stroller with one hand. There are aches and pains and strains of all manner in your future, and, as a doctor once advised as a general guide for men: Until you're twenty-five, it'll get better; after that, get used to it.

The Baby

"As the big day approaches, my anxieties are driving me crazy. I've just got to know that our baby is going to be okay."

Try to relax. You've eaten right, avoided all the problems you could, done everything you could to improve your odds. And while we can't guarantee that your baby will be perfect, we can guarantee that your baby will be ugly. Yup. Ugly is a sure thing when it comes to newborns.

Sure, everyone will coo and say how beautiful the baby is, but most of them are seeing the kid after three or four days of recovery and respiration. You, however, will be face-to-face with this creature the very first moment that he or she looks around and says, "What the . . . !"

As is well known, newborns look like J. Edgar Hoover, Winston Churchill, or, at best, the young Babe Ruth. However, the pudgy, wrinkled, droopy look is the least of it. Here are a few more reasons to keep photography to a minimum until a few days—or at least a few hours—have passed:

- *The caput:* an elegant name for a highly inelegant bump on the noggin.
- *Sugar loaf molding:* another pretty name, but how pretty can elongation of the head possibly be? The passage through the birth canal essentially squishes Baby's head into a point. As conehead Beldar from the classic *Saturday Night Live* sketch might say, "We are from France, feel free to consume mass quantities."
- *Boxer's nose:* says it all.
- *Baby rug syndrome:* In an apparent

effort to hide their baldness, some babies are born with an all-natural bad toupee. This hair, often dark, long, and patchy, will fall out eventually and be replaced by new growth.

- *Lanugo:* Yes, it was a dance sensation from the late 1990s, but it's also patches of downy hair that occur in the oddest places on newborns.
- *Blotches:* Call them angel kisses if it makes you feel better, but there is a whole assortment of potential birthmarks that will keep any baby off the box front of Ivory Snow.
- *Milia:* or, yes, baby acne. Life is unfair, right from the start. At least most teenagers deserve what they get.
- *Receding chin and silly-looking mouth:* Don't worry, teeth will eventually give this area a lot more structure and dignity. Have you seen Gramps without his dentures?

Q. Cold Feet

"I'm really concerned about keeping my cool during the delivery. I've never been too crazy about hospitals, and the sight of blood and IVs—I probably shouldn't go, right?"

A. Many men—indeed many people—feel uncomfortable in the hospital, and around the medical equipment and procedures involved in a modern birth. Perhaps you should consider home birth. We're kidding, of course, but if we scared you, good. Be thankful that you don't have any real responsibility in the hospital. All you have to do is show up, carry a bag or two, and stay out of the nurses' way. It is time to man up!

In many cultures, childbirth is the exclusive province of women. A mother, sister, or female friend is more likely to be present as the pregnant woman's companion. Too bad you don't live in one of those cultures. You will be mocked and ridiculed if you don't accompany your wife to the hospital. Even major-league baseball players now get a special two-day leave when they have a baby, and those guys are about as Neanderthal as it gets. (Not counting hockey players, of course.) But if you are still concerned about being present at the birth, you and your wife should talk it over. Share your feelings, your fears, and your discomfort. Then she can mock and ridicule you, and probably do so on Facebook, too. And you'll still have to go, of course, but maybe she'll forgive you if you proceed to hit the floor at the sight of the crowning head.

CHAPTER ELEVEN

Labor and Delivery

What Your Wife Will Be Complaining About

- Exhaustion
- You
- That willpower has no effect in making irregular contractions become regular
- That you're timing contractions incorrectly
- That it's painful to walk; extremely painful to do anything else
- Pain
- Extreme Pain
- That she can't decide when to go to the hospital
- Your attempt to start her on breathing techniques—it's too soon
- That there's no good reason to get total anesthesia
- That the nurse won't wait for the contraction to end before trying for the third time to hit a vein with the IV
- That medical science has made absolutely no progress on males giving birth
- Mr. Lamaze, whoever he was
- The hospital room
- That she can't believe her ob-gyn is not on call
- Her third-grade art teacher (logic has no meaning to a woman in labor)
- Peer pressure, which is keeping her from taking any and all available anesthetics
- The doctors who don't seem to realize that no one has ever been in this much pain before
- Emotional highs and lows, fear, ecstasy, anxiety, and elation, often all at the same time

It also may not be clear what she's complaining about, because it's so hard to understand her through clenched teeth, but that is definitely not a happy face.

A Couple of Things to Say to Let Her Know You're Caring, Sensitive, and Up On the Required Reading

1. "You know, a prolonged active phase can be caused by a malposition of the baby. It could be a breech, the head hasn't descended into the pelvis, or there is cephalopelvic disproportion—and we all know how much that can hurt, right Honey?"

2. "Until the eighteenth century, women never lay down to give birth; they would walk or stand or squat—all of which are physiologically superior positions. It was the obstetrician to the French court, a doctor named Mauriceau, who introduced the practice of lying down—and the court's standards were widely imitated. I'm sorry, were you having a contraction?"

3. "You know, having the baby hurts, but apparently expelling the placenta afterward doesn't hurt a bit. That's something to be thankful for."

Videotaping Your Delivery

Until hospitals lift their overly conservative policies restricting the delivery room to the woman and her partner or coach, and add stadium-style seating, there is only one way to share the experience of your labor and delivery with family and friends: the magic of digital video.

You could rely on your phone's video, but really the purchase of a video camera is as much a pregnancy tradition as painting the nursery. So don't wait until you bring the baby home to begin the HD documentary drama that is your child's life. And for goodness' sake, neither you nor your wife should be shy about taping these special hours for posterity. The camera may seem intrusive at times, and it's not always easy to think about your laboring wife's needs and keep an eye on the framing at the same time, but the laughs you'll share when you watch with relatives and co-workers will more than make up for any initial feelings of embarrassment.

How to make a quality tape? Thoughtfully, most modern hospital delivery rooms are extremely well lit. Amateur videographers are thus protected from that most common problem of low light. You will probably need a standard video light for the hospital room itself, but once active labor begins—at which time you may be occasionally distracted from your camera

THE POPGAR TEST

With the increased involvement of fathers in the birthing process, with fathers even attending cesarean births, it became necessary to develop a hospital methodology for the fathers. The acronymic POPGAR test has become the norm. This simple test was developed in the late 1980s to help hospital personnel evaluate a father in those critical moments just after the birth of his child. He is rated on a scale of 0, 1, or 2 points, in six areas: pallor, optimism, pride, grimace, activity, and relatives. A total score of 7 or above indicates a healthy father; a low score may indicate a need for more careful observation.

How the POPGAR Test Is Scored

AREA	0	1	2
Pallor	White as a sheet	Washed out	Pale
Optimism	Thinks Baby said "Dada"	Thinks Baby is looking at him	Thinks Baby is beautiful
Pride	Asks nurse if the paparazzi have been bothering her for details	Asks nurse if she's ever seen a more perfect baby	Asks nurse if all babies are so great
Grimace	Slack-jawed	Smiles hazily	Can't stop grinning
Activity	Nods off in a chair	Walks Baby	Dances with Baby
Relatives	Can't remember if he has relatives	He has called the key relatives	Has already updated Facebook status

work—the lighting is all taken care of.

Some expectant fathers worry that they simply cannot function effectively as both cameraman and coach. Well, that's what tripods are for! Should your wife need a quick review of breathing techniques or someone to toss a stray curse at, you can be there—and still be getting it all down on tape. This has the added benefit of allowing you to appear on camera. Unfortunately, the resulting video will be rather static, and you risk losing your audience's full attention. You may want to consider strapping a camcorder to a football helmet to create a perfectly serviceable "Daddy-cam." A ten-dollar remote cable will allow you to operate the PAUSE/RECORD button with your teeth and still have both hands free for brow mopping and back rubbing.

When you're preparing to tape your child's birth, it is best to make everything as idiotproof as possible, because with all the excitement and tension it's easy to forget to charge the batteries or create in-camera graphics. Here are some simple videotaping tips for the delivery room:

- Don't ask the anesthesiologist to hold the microphone.
- Don't ad-lib a humorous voice-over as you shoot. You can add it later.
- Don't try to make the atmosphere seem "more personal" by asking the doctors and nurses to remove their masks.
- Never, ever tell your wife to push harder because you're running out of tape.
- Don't joke with the hospital personnel about the tape being good evidence for your upcoming malpractice suit.
- Don't video cesareans.
- Don't attempt to come up with similes to describe the moments-old newborn. No one wants to consider how much a new infant looks like a skinned rabbit, for example.
- Three hours is too long, even if you're planning to edit it down, and you'll never get around to editing it down, anyway.
- Please, please, please ignore all of the above and anything in this book, or in any book, that suggests you videotape your wife's delivery. First, most hospitals won't let you. Second, you don't want to do this, trust me. Third, sure, there may be some things you'd like to remember in labor and delivery, but there will also be a lot more you'd want to forget.

In the News: The Latest Reports

Up to this point, this compendium of helpful guidance for expectant fathers has indulged in some obvious fictions, for comic effect. But proving that truth is stranger than fiction, what follows is genuine information. Through diligent research, we found these tidbits of reality, about fathering in general, as well as the latest options in pregnancy, labor, and delivery, for you to consider.

NOT SO XX

The *New York Times* deemed it front-page news when scientists reported in 2011 that a man's testosterone levels measurably decrease after he becomes a father. "And the more he gets involved in caring for his children—changing diapers, jiggling the boy or girl on his knee, reading *Goodnight Moon* for the umpteenth time—the lower his testosterone drops." (Frankly, we find this unfairly demonizes *Goodnight Moon*. After all, *Pat the Bunny* is far more emasculating.) Some observers immediately suggested that the lesson was that parenting was very important, in that it impacted our physiology. No one suggested, unfortunately, that this provided a legitimate medical reason for why men should not change diapers.

MALE CRAVINGS?

"We are for the first time asking men: Does becoming a father affect your hor-mones?" said Dr. Katherine Wynne-Edwards of Queen's University in Canada. "And the answer is: 'Yes it does.'" The Canadian researcher tested men during the months when their wives were expecting and discovered increases in estrogenlike hormones along with decreases in testosterone. These physiological changes were judged to be substantial enough to cause weight gain, morning sickness, and even food cravings.

INVITE FLIPPER

As reported in *USA Today* under the headline "Dolphin Births Nixed," a group of six British women were denied permission to deliver their babies in a special glass-walled water tank in the Red Sea. Their obstetrician hoped that being born among dolphins would give the infants a special affinity with nature and might improve human–dolphin communication. No specific reason was reported for the denial. I'd guess maybe it was that the applicants were judged to be nutbars.

INVITE THE NEIGHBORS

Unlike modern America, where laboring women are sequestered in hospitals, other societies have made birth a pleasant social affair. Family and friends—including children—gather to offer moral support for the young mother to be. Imagine all your nearest and dearest cheering you on through the entire labor and birth. It's good to be a repressed American.

ROUGH 'EM UP!

In case you're feeling marginalized by the whole mothercentric birth process, just bide your time. ABC News reported that Australian researchers have determined that fathers roughhousing with kids plays a key developmental role. Hooray, one for our side! The physical rough-and-tumble games allow children to combine their physical, social, and mental capabilities in ways other games don't. The ability to "defeat" an adult builds confidence, while having an adult withhold his superior strength builds trust. Frankly, I'm all for arguments that fathers are important, but this particular report seemed rather vague. As far as I can tell, these scientists sat around watching dads and toddlers wrestle over a sock, and then speculated about what they were learning. Just saying.

TECHNOLOGY FROM NASA

Though the system is not particularly popular, some countries have allowed the use of a special decompression suit for the laboring mother. This suit lifts the abdomen away from the uterus during each contraction. The decrease in pressure on the uterus allows it to work more effectively, which means less pain for the mother.

ONLY IN SWEDEN

An innovation in natural childbirth has been pioneered in Sweden. Doctors there have found that using a Japanese-made cervical vibrator as often as three times during the first stage of labor allows the cervix to relax between contractions. This, in turn, allows the cervix to work more effectively with the contraction. Add your own joke here.

THE REVOLUTION WILL BE TELEVISED

In certain segments of the market research done by the Nielsen ratings, a pregnant woman is statistically considered to be two viewers. It may seem strange, but for the marketers of baby and child care products—diapers, toys, rug cleaners—this is a valid measurement of the impact their television commercials are having; so your wife is, quantitatively speaking, watching for two.

WHAT YOU MAY BE CONCERNED ABOUT

Fear Of Switching

Q. "I watch a lot of made-for-television movies. I guess what I'm trying to get at is that, well, I know it's probably ridiculous, but I'm terrified the hospital will somehow switch our baby."

A. No fear that you are feeling is ridiculous, but you should be reassured by the simple fact that only one in ten babies born in this country is accidentally switched with another at the hospital. Nonetheless, fear of a switch crosses the mind of almost every new parent. Did we say one in ten? We meant one in ten million births; and actually, we just made up that figure, but it's probably some really big number like ten or twenty million. (Although, logically, it would have to be two in ten million, because if one got switched, then there must be another one that got switched, too.)

That said, it is still worth putting your mind at ease by taking a few simple precautions as soon as your child is born. Sure, they have the coordinating mom-and-baby bracelets, but somehow that only adds to the sense of doubt. After all, the hospitals wouldn't have instituted the bracelet system if they weren't a little unsure of themselves, right? True story: One father we know spent a few moments bonding with his newborn, and after deciding that he couldn't lock in on any particular distinguishing feature, he took a moment to put a discreet black x on his child's foot. Sure, the nurses were a little mystified, and his wife teased him relentlessly, but at least he came home with *his* baby. An indelible marker, a friendship bracelet, a quick haircut, whatever you do, don't rely on memorizing your baby's features. He may look unique at that first moment, but your perspective will be a little different when you're behind the glass of the hospital nursery looking at a whole roomful of swaddled newborns with squishy little faces.

Painkillers

Q. *"We're getting so much information about all the various options for pain relief—epidurals, analgesics, hypnosis—that it's dizzying. Aren't there any simple answers?"*

A. Unfortunately, the process of labor and childbirth is a complicated matter, with many possibilities and probabilities to be considered. You may experience severe tension headaches, back strain, and even red, irritated eyes. When giving a back massage, you may find that your hands cramp up. When you nod off in a chair, your leg may fall asleep, which can lead to a painful tingling when you try to use it. It can't be denied: Childbirth involves pain.

Ideally, your childbirth preparation classes have taught you not to fear the pain. Though many of those one-sided classes tend to focus on women's issues, the same basic principles apply to you. Concentrate on your breathing. Use the pain; don't fight it so much as try to go with it. Most of all, relax as much as you can, whenever you can. If you can nod off between your wife's contractions, that's great.

Still, there may come a time for medical intervention, and you shouldn't feel bullied into refusing it. Pay no attention to men who say that with medication you aren't "really experiencing" childbirth. These militant anti–medical establishment types will tell you that a man's body was created with the ability to stand idly by while a woman is giving birth, without any help from doctors and medication. Make your own decision. If you decide you need a couple of aspirin for the headache, take them, by all means. (And bring your own, because the hospital won't give out any medication to nonpatients.) Feel free to do whatever you can to ease the pain during the long hours of labor and the intense pressure of childbirth. (No, not getting drunk. Sheesh.) You deserve a little help in getting through it.

What to Say During Labor

Q. *"We took the classes, I've read the books, and I'm still not exactly sure what I'm supposed to say or do as labor coach, except that it has something to do with a tennis ball."*

A. Many men go into labor—so to speak—terrified of saying the wrong thing and, in the midst of labor, are bored of saying the same thing over and over. And the tennis ball—suggested as a means of massaging the lower back—seldom actually comes into play. Neither does the giant blue yoga exercise ball that she made you carry into the hospital fully inflated.

What can you do? It's really not that complicated. First, you are your wife's willing slave, jumping at her every whim.

Second, you are an interpreter between your wife and the hospital personnel, explaining to her what they are suggesting, and translating her grunts and snarls into relatively polite discourse. Third is the coaching part—and don't worry, the nurses handle the nitty-gritty. You didn't really think that you would be the one to make the call on when active labor has begun, or when to administer an epidural, did you? So don't worry about keeping an eye on the readouts from the fetal monitor—unless you'd like to stare at them and experiment with self-hypnosis. Plus, the nurses most likely know all the breathing gimmicks better than you do. So all you really have to do is provide encouragement and love. How? Stick to the basics and, if in doubt, remember that, especially as labor progresses, less is more. Chitchat may only annoy her. Occasional eye contact may be all she wants. You're nothing but a target for her glowering.

What to Say to Your Wife During Early (First-Phase) Labor

1. "Everything is packed and ready to go."
2. "I love you."
3. "I bought you a little present—just for being a wonderful person."
4. "I just have a feeling it's going to go smoothly."
5. Sing the complete lyrics to Paul Anka's "(You're) Having My Baby" while her sense of humor is still

functioning. (Although, strictly speaking, she should sing the second verse—which is an answer to the male voice of the first verse.)

6. "It must have been that Chinese food."
7. "I hope she looks like you."
8. "Just try to relax as much as you can."

What *Not* to Say to Your Wife During Early (First-Phase) Labor

1. "Just relax as much as you can—labor can go on for days."
2. "This isn't another bogus false labor thing, is it?"
3. "I forget, which hospital is it again?"
4. "Either my stopwatch is broken or the contractions are slowing down."
5. "Can't we wait a little longer before we go to the hospital? It's the fourth quarter."
6. "Don't forget, this is the easy part."
7. "I just can't wait to have that baby."

What to Say to Your Wife During Active (Second-Phase) Labor

1. "I love you."
2. "That's great."
3. "Good, beautiful."
4. "You're wonderful."
5. "Sure it does."
6. "You're doing great."
7. "Relax between contractions—that's it."
8. "You can do it."
9. "You're strong."
10. "Is there anything at all you want?"

What *Not* to Say to Your Wife During Active (Second-Phase) Labor

1. "You don't look like you're having fun." (Irony might play during first-phase labor, but lose it for active labor.)
2. "You're not as relaxed as you should be." (Negativity.)
3. "I can't bear to see you in so much pain." (She needs strength, not pity.)
4. "I just figured out in my head how much this hospital is costing us per minute."
5. "You had the baby! Ha! Made you look."
6. "You think this is tough? Larry's wife was in labor for forty-three hours."
7. "Mind if I nap until the action starts?"

What to Say to Your Wife During Transitional (Third-Phase) Labor

1. "It's okay, you're okay."
2. "I love you."
3. "You're wonderful."
4. "You're working hard."
5. "You're doing great."
6. "Remember, just relax between contractions—don't anticipate the next one."
7. "We've waited a long time—and that baby's not that far away now."

What *Not* to Say to Your Wife During Transitional (Third-Phase) Labor

1. "A friend of mine who's a doctor said that physiological evidence shows that labor ranks right up there with gunshot wounds on the pain scale."
2. "I've heard that there's a kind of hormonal amnesia so that women don't remember just how painful labor was."
3. "Do you think I look nice in the hospital regulation outfit?"
4. "Once I broke my wrist, and that sure hurt."
5. "I can't believe you haven't even broken your water yet."
6. "I've been having some second thoughts about the name we decided on."
7. "Don't blame me—it's nature."
8. "Do you ever wonder how competent all these doctors and technicians are? I mean, they must have all done it for the first time at some point, you know?"
9. "Well, if you're not going to breathe with me, I'm just not going to bother breathing at all."

What to Say to Your Wife During Pushing, Delivery, and After

1. Nothing until after—she's not listening.
2. "You did it."
3. "You're wonderful."
4. "I love you."
5. "Look at our baby boy/girl."
6. "Thank you."

What *Not* to Say to Your Wife During Pushing, Delivery, and After

1. "It's great that you're not worried about your modesty anymore."
2. "Look at what a mess this place is."
3. "You know what's another good name for a girl? Sylvia—isn't that a pretty name?"
4. "Eww—that's the baby?"
5. "Yes, I did it!"
6. "When can we have another one?"
7. "What a minute, that baby looks like Phil, our garage mechanic."
8. "How many days do you think you want to stay—two, three?"
9. "What should I do with all the dirty laundry at home?"

Taking Pictures

Q. *"Okay, you talked me out of videotaping our upcoming birth, but I'd like to take some photographs. Are there any problems with still photography in hospitals?"*

A. Our advice is quite simple: Take your camera to the hospital, but do not take any pictures until one full hour after the birth of your child. Any photographs of your wife in labor will not be appreciated: Photographs of deliveries are best confined to pregnancy guides and medical textbooks, and newborns look a lot better once they've had a little breathing room. If you truly feel the first moments outside the womb need to be documented, fine, but keep it to a minimum. Moments like these are too important to spend behind a lens. Also, go with high-speed film or set the digital on NO FLASH so that you can minimize glare in your baby's eyes during the first hours of life. This is not for physiological reasons but for psychological ones. Taking too many photos can put the hour-old child at risk of contracting IPS—infant paparazzo syndrome—a nonthreatening condition marked by an inflated sense of importance.

While we're on the subject, once you do begin taking hundreds and hundreds of digital photographs, please remember that, while it is very easy in this digital age to send everyone you know all 574 photos of Junior (and because it happened to be in the same grouping, the seven shots of the leak above the kitchen you took for insurance purposes), it is not very considerate. Take that extra time to pick and choose. Thank you. From all of us.

Circumcision

Q. *"I always assumed that circumcision was done for medical reasons, but now I hear that it is no longer considered particularly beneficial."*

A. Fathers who have attended their baby's circumcision are usually shocked to see what he has to go through. They often feel guilt and anguish over having authorized the procedure, which is a very good reason not to go and watch. Do you really want to see your newborn son placed in a "circumstraint" and see a hemostat applied, clamps, and . . . you don't even want to read about it.

Does it hurt? Are you kidding? It hurts just thinking about it. Some people tell themselves that the infant's nervous system is not fully developed. These people are fooling themselves. For certainly most male infants wail for all they're worth when the deed is done.

Is it worth doing? There is slim evidence of any medical advantages. The most common reason that 65 percent of American parents still choose circumcision is that 65 percent of American parents still choose circumcision. This fear of looking different may be unfortunate, but it is not unreasonable. Looking different can be confusing for a young boy. The argument, based solely on aesthetics, that somehow it just looks better, is a cover for the fact that

65 percent of baby boys start life with a little trim. And a few decades ago, that figure was 80 percent, so circumcision is generally on the decline. You may find that your medical team actively discourages it. If you'd like to get embroiled in impassioned debate about the virtue of an "intact" penis and the "mutilation" of our men-children, feel free to hop on the Internet, where there is sure to be a message board that will thoroughly tick you off, whichever side you take.

Of course, you may be Jewish. If you're not sure, don't worry about it. If you are, circumcision is more than just a little hospital procedure; it's a bris. This means you must wait the traditional eight days and then have a mohel come remove in a special service what the forefathers had removed. (Or should it be foreless-fathers?) Relatives and friends gather in joyous celebration, complete with lox-and-bagel platters, while the little fellow and his mother are in the back bedroom sobbing. By the way, if you're Christian and feeling left out, you could celebrate the Circumcision (of Jesus, that is), which is January 1, although not many churches hold special services. And if they did, what exactly would they be praying for?

Rumors and speculation about circumcision's role in human sexuality are common, but unfounded. It has never been proven that circumcised men can hold an erection longer, nor has it been proven that uncircumcised men experience greater sexual pleasure, although a government-funded group of researchers at Cornell University had a hell of a good time trying to find out.

CHAPTER TWELVE

The First Weeks

What Your Wife Will Be Complaining About

- Exhaustion
- You
- That she still looks pregnant even though Baby is out
- That she will never walk again—despite nurses' continued "you'll recover faster," urging her to try
- Perineal pain
- Fear of postpartum depression (technically known as pre-postpartum depression)
- Fear of bowel movements
- Sore nipples if breast-feeding
- Whoever invented breast-feeding in the first place
- Your family's ill-timed visits, goofy gifts, and passive-aggressive comments
- The flowers—she doesn't want to leave any behind
- That the nurses are intrusive and patronizing
- That the nurses are never available and won't tell her anything
- That she did all the work; yet you seem to get half the credit
- That she initially felt Baby was the most gorgeous cherub ever but the realization of Baby's plug-ugliness is dawning
- Baby's belly button stump, which she finds really gross
- That Baby is already too big for the Philadelphia Eagles jumper you bought, although it's probably just as well
- The name you agreed on, which suddenly seems all wrong
- That Social Security already insists on giving your baby a number—it's creepy
- Emotional highs and lows, fear, ecstasy, anxiety, and elation, often all at the same time

A Couple of Things to Say to Let Her Know You're Caring, Sensitive, and Up On the Required Reading

1. "Hey look, I know what that is, that's meconium!"

2. "Sure, our baby looks a little yellow, but it's just mild jaundice. Thank goodness he doesn't have hemolytic jaundice from blood incompatibility—which could damage the nervous system."

3. "Watch—I can get the baby to do the Moro reflex, just by dropping her."

4. "Did you know that the discovery of the hand—a baby noticing its own hand—is one of the essential steps toward psychomotor coordination?"

What Did You Expect?

It may come as a shock, but when you get home from the hospital, you'll quickly realize that being pregnant was the easy part, especially for you, the expectant father. Oh, sure, there were a lot of inconveniences, minor aches and pains, nettlesome planning, and some baby furniture to assemble, but none of it can compare with the early days of fatherhood.

Pregnancy is neat and contained; fatherhood is all over the place. The baby's in the bassinet, the bottles are boiling, the baby needs a change, your wife would love a cup of tea, the baby needs a change, no, not the lemon tea, the herbal raspberry, the two A.M. feeding, the four A.M. feeding, the desperate five A.M. drive around the block, the baby needs a change and in the middle of it puts on a stunning free-form aerial peeing demonstration and now both the baby and you need a change, "Good morning, we're out of coffee," how could the baby need a change I just changed the baby, time to make the doughnuts. And off to work with you, with only a little "cottage cheese" on your shoulder.

You suddenly feel nostalgic for morning sickness. Remember when days would go by without much more than an "Oh, feel here, Honey, she's kicking!" or an awkward attempt to give a back rub to someone who is all front? And when you went to sleep, you could sleep until morning. It didn't even seem that special, sleeping till morning. You know, just close your eyes, drift off, and wake up in the morning. "Good night, see you in the morning." Just one night! Just one night straight through! Is that so much to ask?

Relax. Sleep deprivation, with its attendant psychoses and hallucinations, is a perfectly natural part of early parenting. Many experts on early childhood and parenting experts agree that only by this "disassociation from reality" can the parent survive the trauma of the first six months. It is actually a functional phenomenon.

The Silver Linings of Sleeplessness

The single greatest issue that other parents will warn you about is the lack of sleep. Several well-meaning people will e-mail you the *Go the F**k to Sleep* book, which might seem outrageous when you first get it, but you'll see. There is no doubt that learning to function with interrupted and insufficient sleep is a challenge. Imagine being just a bit drunk all the time. (Imagine, please.) There is a sort of haze, a lack of clarity and attention. You may find yourself irritable and short-tempered. What to do? The answer is to apply the power of positive thinking! Why not spend those "extra" hours of being awake trying to focus on all the good things that come from a lack of sleep! You will no doubt come up with your own, but here are just a few thought starters:

1. Hallucinations are kind of interesting.

2. You don't have to worry about being unshaven, because the bristly look fits so nicely with the dark circles under your eyes.

3. (In stage whisper) "I can't hear too well—can we talk about it later?"

4. You can't do many chores while walking around carrying a baby.

5. It's nice to sleep on the couch for some other reason than your failings as a husband.

6. You can't do enough math in your head to realize how impossible it will be to get through the month/buy a house/pay for college/retire. (Pick your own anxiety.)

7. Telemarketers lose interest in your conversations.

8. Late-night TV is better than it used to be. Even without volume—or the baby will never fall asleep.

9. Places that once seemed far too uncomfortable for napping seem to work just fine: living room floor, back of a cab, in a church pew, on the can, in the garage, or in the conference room during office staff meetings.

10. You're too tired to resent that your wife is too tired.

Crying

Q. *"Crying at night, crying first thing in the morning, I can't take it anymore—and the baby cries a lot, too. And what should I do when the baby and wife are both crying? Who should I go to first?"*

A. As the prerecorded airline announcement wisely says, please affix your own oxygen mask before helping others. There, now, take a deep breath. You might think that babies cry all the time and that a crying adult would always be first priority, but think again. If you go to your wife to console her, the howling of the baby will only make you both so tense and anxious that you'll end up snapping, "Quit blubbering," and she'll say, "You don't deserve a family because you don't care about anyone but yourself," and the baby will still be screaming like a banshee with a hot foot, and your wife will say, "Just go away, you make me sick," and you'll say, "Nothing would make me happier," and then you'll go get the baby finally, and your wife will still be crying or possibly calling her mother, and it turns out that the baby had her arm stuck in the side of the crib, and now you feel really bad, the baby hates you, the wife hates you, and you've got to get up in the morning and head into a corporate headquarters where there

are at least a handful of people who also hate you or who are, at best, angling for your job. So if you're still concerned about crying, yes, it's okay to cry. As long as no one sees you.

Taking Care of Mom

Q. *"I run my own business and can't afford to stay home from work for too long, but I want to take good care of my wife, too."*

A. More and more, men are able to be at home during those first weeks, thanks to paternity leave specifically and male enlightenment in general, but for some it won't be possible. If your wife buys into your particular excuse, you're past the biggest hurdle, but you'll still want to arrange some kind of help for her.

The first option is, of course, her mom. You probably don't have much choice in this matter. If they've worked it out, Mom will be waiting on the doorstep when you bring the baby home. If you've never appreciated your mother-in-law, you will now. An extra nap and a warm meal never looked so good. You'll probably forgive her for everything. Of course, when the baby is learning to walk, it might be time to suggest politely that she is pushing the limits of her welcome.

Another option is your mom. Just kidding.

Finally, if you can afford the luxury, look for a doula service. *Doula* is a word of Greek origin meaning "to mother the mother," which seems like a lot of idea for two syllables, but then those Greeks have a very impressive-looking alphabet. The people who provide this service are usually RNs or LPNs, but in addition to taking care of the baby and instructing the new mom, they are a sympathetic companion for her, do light housekeeping, even cooking and laundry. It's pricey, but if you can't be there yourself, assuage your guilt and fork over the moolah for the doula.

Q. Hair Loss

"Maybe I'm imagining it, but I think I'm losing hair more rapidly."

A. There is still disagreement in the medical community over this issue. Pregnancy—and postpartum in particular—is a traumatic period for the father, both emotionally and physically. Could this cause hair loss and accelerated balding?

Women in the postpartum period will also suffer hair loss, but this is definitely a temporary physiological experience. High hormone levels during pregnancy cause hairs that would ordinarily fall out to stay. Her hair will get thicker throughout the nine months, but with childbirth, decreases in those hormone levels will cause the extra hair to fall out. This is a natural process that may be shocking, but it does not lead to baldness.

In men the news is not so cheery. Hair loss is hair loss, like it or not. Could trauma be at the root of the problem? Most scientists believe that balding is solely determined by genetics, others believe that physical and emotional factors have an effect, and a small minority believe that tiny hair elves come and pluck at the scalps of men who have been bad.

There is hope. The national epidemic of balding is beginning to get the public attention and scientific funding it deserves. Many old theories of balding are now being tested in research labs. The it's-determined-by-your-mother's-father's-hair genetic theory has been disproved by the author. My forehead is ever heightening, while my maternal grandfather sported his shock of dignified white hair all of his seventy-seven years. The promulgators of such theories should think twice about the false confidence they inspire—and about our broken hearts, for cripes' sake.

Other theories have also been put to rest. Does hat wearing cause baldness? Definitely not, although researchers have established that balding does cause hat wearing. Conspiracy theorists who believe that Hair Club for Men has put something into the nation's water supply have yet to produce hard evidence.

Rogaine and other medicines have now been proven effective, but if you are planning on having more babies, chances are you want to stay away from any elective medications and chemicals. How can something that can grow hair not have an impact on your genetic chemical makeup?

Our advice is not to worry too much. You'll still have more hair than the baby, for a few months anyway.

Going Back to Work

"We are having the whole working versus staying-at-home debate—can we afford day care? What are the best options? Will spending all day with nothing but kids be mind numbing? Will time away be a major career setback? Will we feel like the kids are being raised by a nanny? It all comes down to one question: Should I go back to work?"

Yes. You have to.

Working Woman

"Okay, but what about my wife?"

Ah, pregnancy! America's favorite short-term disability! Many women, especially first-time mothers, are working and expecting at the same time. Stacking up pregnancy leave, vacations, and personal days gets the majority of women two or three months, but most of that will be sensibly devoted to the postbirth time frame. That leaves you with an increasingly pregnant wife trundling off to the office (unless she is in a career in which pregnancy calls for a more immediate halt: firefighter, tree surgeon, fashion model, arctic explorer, or competitive eater).

Being partner to a woman balancing her career and pregnancy calls for special sensitivity, and thus you are bound to fail. Still, let's see what we can do. First, do not focus on the potential loss of her income. No matter what the specifics are in the balance of your breadwinning, your best bet is to leave the choice completely up to her. Unpaid leave, deciding to stay home, passing up promotions, avoiding work travel assignments, playing the lottery, moving to some tiny upstate town where real estate is dirt cheap, whatever she wants, you want, too. There will be plenty of time to talk her out of it later.

Sure, that's easy enough. Next question from your wife: "Why don't you make more money?" Plenty of answers leap to mind. Sarcasm is best kept to inner monologue—*Because I'm an idiot. Because I don't try hard. What would I want more money for? I'm still secretly paying off mob blackmailers.* So what is the right answer? If you know, please contact me as soon as possible: Thomas Hill, c/o Andrews McMeel Publishing, 1130 Walnut Street, Kansas City, Missouri 64106-2109.

A pregnant wife's career has many benefits besides the obvious economic one. Working women have less time to scour the Internet for rare pregnancy issues and less time to chat with other neighborhood women about the sorry state of your local public schools. Going to work will also prevent the complete surrender to schlubby clothes or even pajamas. Not that they aren't cute, but all day every day?

After the baby is born, working mothers . . . wait, I take that phrase back! All mothers are working mothers! Being home with a baby or kids is exhausting and demanding. After the baby is born, "mothers who are returning to the workplace" face many disparate challenges. For many, it is a welcome return to a career they find energizing and self-affirming. For others, it is a difficult transition. They would rather be at home with their baby. Paid work is hard, tedious, tiring, or worse. Guess which one is trouble for you? And what exactly is keeping you from asking Mr. Dithers for a raise?

Fear of Changing

"I don't like changing diapers. Can we start toilet training now that the baby is a week old?"

No, you may not, you sniveling wimp. You're so far away from toilet training, it's funny. But the most feared task in fathering is also the most overrated. Changing diapers is no big deal. In the first two years of your baby's life, you will become completely inured to many grosser tasks. If you want something to feed your nightmares, try these:

- You take the baby's temperature with the rectal thermometer.
- You suck snot out of the baby's nose with a nasal aspirator.
- We don't even want to talk about it—but it has to do with constipation.
- You catch vomit in your hand, because you didn't have a spit-up diaper handy.
- You blow Baby's nose with your bare hand, using either a discreet fling or a sock for disposal.
- You use your own former toothbrush in an effort to clean a wicker chair that met up with an insufficient diaper.

It would be needlessly alarmist to go into great detail about the potential disasters that loom, but we must give one simple warning: Never play "flying baby" while lying on your back with your mouth open right after the baby has been fed.

The Name

"I can't get used to the name we gave this baby. It just doesn't seem to be sticking. Is it possible we picked the wrong name?"

Many new parents can't get used to the idea that they are empowered to give this new creature a name. Assigning a name, after all, is a quintessential expression of dominance. Adam—the first man—was given the awesome task of naming all the other creatures.

If you knew your baby's gender and picked a name months ago, it may seem more natural to you. It is simply a matter of finally making a formal introduction. But if you're one of those who waited, laying a name on this baby may seem impossible. What if Baby doesn't like it?

Have you really chosen the wrong name? Impossible! You considered, you debated, you settled on the name you both thought was right. Stick with it. (Actually, it is statistically possible—about one in twenty thousand—that you have chosen a name so bad that it actually is wrong, like Phlegma or Tohmas. In these cases, the courts are very lenient and allow name changes with a minimum of legal entanglements.) The name

you have chosen is the right one, but getting used to it can still be difficult. A silly nickname is often the answer. By calling your infant Fluffernutter or Baldy for a while, you can adjust yourself to the idea that the little ball of pudge is Cynthia, Gilbert, or Ariadne. And if you never really do get used to the name, the worst thing that can happen is that you'll end up with a twenty-five-year-old son in medical school who still goes by the name Wizzer.

Wisdom of the Fathers

"Now that the baby is here and happy and healthy, I've got a whole new set of anxieties. Number one is: Who am I to teach this little human all about the meaning of life?"

You've learned to be a decent friend: concerned, engaging, sympathetic. You've started learning to be a decent spouse: sharing, loving, supportive. But a father has to be all that and also *wise*. That is a tall order for the best of us. Whether you have any wisdom to offer or not, someday your child will ask—expecting reasonably complete, comprehensible answers—if dogs go to heaven, why there is war, why some people are poor, why Aunt Susan never got married, why they are allowed to sell cigarettes if they're bad for you, why it isn't stealing when you take envelopes and paper from the office. And you thought "Why is the sky blue?" and "What are belly buttons for?" were tough!

How can you prepare for the interrogations? There are a few simple plans. Misdirection can work: "Presto! What's this? A quarter in your ear!" Deflection is fairly reliable: "Ask your mother." But ultimately, you're going to have to bite the bullet and accept responsibility for the fact that you have led a fairly unexamined life. If you're a churchgoer, you've got a good head start on the rest of us heathens. If not, now would be a good time to get in touch with your spiritual side, wrestle with some ethical issues, and decide what your purpose on Earth is. You'll need something to ponder while you're walking back and forth with a squalling baby on your shoulder. You've actually got at least six or seven years before the ethical/philosophical questions start to crop up. Then you can explain that 55 MPH is sort of a "general guideline," and that you're really not quite sure why only Noah and Mrs. Noah and two of each animal got to live through the flood, while *all* the fish must have survived.

In a related matter, in case you're worried about "the talk," here's one simple approach: Go full bore with the antiquated birds and bees, pollen and stamens metaphor explanation. Not to save yourself embarrassment, mind you, but you would hate to spoil the surprise of the sixth-grade health class films, right?

Finally, if you're really concerned from a philosophical perspective about the influence you will have on your children, just read up on the latest counterintuitive sociological research that shows that, ultimately, parents are one of the least influential factors in raising good kids. You rank well behind "peers" and just slightly ahead of "astrological sign." So rest easy; even the wisest counsel and most philosophically sound and elegantly crafted maxims will go in one ear and out the other.

The Balloons

Q. *"Aren't balloons a major health hazard for little kids? What am I supposed to do with all these 'It's a Boy' balloons?"*

A. Over the coming years, you'll be told by intrusive strangers that you are irresponsible and a bad parent for such crimes as letting your kids play with balloons, having popcorn, flinging them in the air, or not brushing their hair out of their eyes. The best response is always to act as though they have single-handedly saved your child's life with their advice and reformed you as a parent forever. That seems to be what they are expecting.

The potential danger of balloons is that a popped balloon can be swallowed or inhaled, and the rubber is particularly hard for doctors to locate. However, you will also find that kids love balloons. Denied, they may become an obsession. All the more reason that Mylar "It's a Boy/Girl" helium balloons have completely replaced traditional rubber or synthetic balloons. Better still, these extraordinary inventions last up to five hundred times longer. In fact, some of these Mylar balloons have become family heirlooms, passed on, still aloft, from generation to generation.

Q. Child Care

"Life is so complicated with the new baby here, I haven't had time to begin looking for a live-in nanny. And, of course, we're concerned about making a good choice."

A. Ah, yes. You're having trouble finding just the right fully qualified and trustworthy candidate for the full-time child-care position? What do you want? Sympathy? Why don't you have the butler make a few phone calls for you, set up some interviews with your personal secretary, and once they've got it down to two or three candidates, you can set down your drink by the pool and come inside for long enough to pick one. That shouldn't be too much of a strain.

Actually, perhaps we're not being entirely fair. Today, more and more women with middle-class incomes find that they must go back to work so that they can afford to pay for full-time child care. Hmmm . . . but if . . . all right, that's still not fair because many women do need to work for economic reasons, and any woman certainly has the right to combine work and motherhood.

The choice between being a working mother and working as a mother is a difficult one, and the two camps are breaking out into what has become a national "Mommy War."* Women on both sides try to keep an open mind but simply have no idea how the other side could possibly have made such a limiting, impractical, and essentially wrong decision. What is the husband's role? We'll give you a clue. It is *not* to carefully consider and weigh the pluses and minuses of each position. All right, we'll give you another clue. *Don't* even come close to forming an opinion until your wife has made up her mind, then totally agree with her. There's a war going on out there, and loose lips sink ships.

* Note the incredibly careful way I have phrased this to avoid any implication that being at home with the children is anything less than full-time work.

CHAPTER THIRTEEN

Life with Baby

What Your Wife Will Be Complaining About

- Exhaustion
- You
- That Baby smiled at her but everyone insists it's just gas
- Sleep deprivation
- Breast-feeding—though easier now, it's still not exactly fun
- Breast pump
- Spit-up
- Diapers
- Fears of inadequacy as a mother
- Hospital bills, paperwork
- Inadequacy of local public schools
- The injustice of it all
- That after all those years of *Conan* being on way too late, now it's over way too early
- The high cost of college education
- That clipping a baby's fingernails is terrifying
- That baby's beautiful blue eyes are quickly fading to brown
- Ridiculously high-pressure and totally unnecessary educational programs (French for Tots, Math Readiness, Baby Swimmers, etc.)
- Expense of all of these programs
- Difficulty of scheduling all of these programs
- Birthmark that "would fade" but hasn't
- That the doctor gave the baby an "outie"
- That black-and-white high-contrast educational toys may be pedagogically sound, but they're ugly
- Too many stuffed animals already (just wait, more are on the way)
- That prolonged exposure to babies is making the adult sections of her brain atrophy
- Designated-hitter rule (okay, but wouldn't it be cool if she did?)
- Emotional highs and lows, fear, ecstasy, anxiety, and elation, often all at the same time

A Couple of Things to Say to Let Her Know You're Caring, Sensitive, and Up On the Required Reading

Remember, these suggestions are based on actual scientific studies.

1. "You know, another good reason breast-feeding is preferable to the bottle is that breast milk has twice as much taurine, a nonprotein nitrogen compound, as there is in cow's milk (which is what most formulas are made of). Taurine seems to be a necessary neurotransmitter or neuromodulator, and not only do babies have a limited enzymatic capacity for synthesizing taurine from precursors, but premature infants have been shown to have high concentrations of taurine in their blood, and I don't have to tell you what that means. Do I? And by the way, taurine is the same ingredient that Red Bull touts on the can, so really what they're selling is breast milk with caffeine."

2. "Projectile vomiting—that is, vomiting that travels some distance away from the baby—though a bit terrifying, isn't a sure sign of a problem unless it happens frequently, once or twice every day."

3. "While constipation is a common problem in babies, it is very treatable, with the very rare exception of Hirschsprung's disease, a total constipation caused by malfunctioning intestinal muscles. I wonder if Mrs. Hirschsprung thought it was a good idea to give it the family name?"

4. "Did you know that more pediatricians are now warning against teaching babies to swim, not because of the danger of drowning, but because of the danger of water intoxication, which happens when a baby—who doesn't know any better—drinks large amounts of water while in the pool, causing potentially serious imbalances internally."

What to Buy During the First Year

Just because you've been spending money all pregnancy long doesn't mean you can quit now. There's so much more your child needs, today!

ESTIMATED COSTS, THE FIRST YEAR

Basics: $1,235
  (Does not include either diaper service at $90 per month or disposables at $125 per month)
Basics plus extras: $6,285

Basics
  Baby sunglasses
  French for Tots
  Gymboree classes
  Home hair-cutting kit
  Infant CPR classes, for you
  Music time
  Name in hand-tooled wood blocks
  Professional portrait photos
  Shoelace clamps (keeps 'em tied)
  Spillproof Cheerios/raisin dispenser
  Toddler leash
  Wee Playhouse acting workshops

Extras
  Baby's own business cards
  Baby's own iPad (yeah, at first it seemed cute that he could play on yours)
  Dog for Baby
  Horseback riding lessons
  Nicer pajamas/bathrobe—since you're wearing them out of the house when you're on hopeful sleep-inducing drives
  Tree house
  Smartphone apps to download *Blue's Clues* snippets to use as emergency distractions

Total Childproofing

Making your home safe for your child isn't as complicated as you may believe. Yes, there are childproofing services that will survey your home and make recommendations and installations, but nothing they do takes more than a little research, a bit of common sense, and the most basic carpentry. Sure, there are whole catalogs full of childproofing equipment, but you need to buy only what your home requires. How much does your home require? Where should you draw the line on childproofing? The final decision is your own.

There are certain basics that should be considered essential—outlet plugs, doorway gates, locks for the kitchen cabinets—beyond these items, each couple needs to find a level of comfort. If additional gates and baby monitors in every room, and an edge padding all around the coffee table, and special bolts to keep the flat-screen from tipping make you feel secure, and thus help you relax, then they've accomplished something before your baby even comes home from the hospital.

Whenever you are purchasing toys, crayons, markers, clay, glue, soap, shampoo, ointments, or anything that is marked "nontoxic," do what I do. Take a moment to think about the poor rats that had to subsist on it for three months to make sure. It only seems fair.

In the meantime, if you know you want total childproofing you can call in consultants—they're in your local yellow pages—or do it yourself with the following products:

The Kitchen: Where Disaster Lurks

DISHWASHER "DUMMY" CONTROL PANEL: Because these controls are by far the most fascinating to the toddler, it may be worth installing a false front with knobs and levers they can adjust at will.

FLOOR STUBBIES: Small rubber knobs glued onto the floor add traction to otherwise slick linoleum.

COMBINATION LOCK KNIFE BLOCK: A simple four-number code allows you to remove knives.

CHILDPROOF DOG/CAT FOOD DISH: Miracle electronic sensory device prevents your child from tasting Spot's dinner but allows the pooch to eat at will. (Warning: It will not function properly if your child has whiskers.)

The Bathroom

CHILDPROOF TOILET LID: This lid makes the toilet safe for kids, and it's lots of fun at parties, when increasingly anxious guests can't figure out the "simple" four-step unlocking mechanism.

GENTLE FLUSH SYSTEM: The patented commode soundproofing cushions and minimizes the loud and potentially frightening sound of the toilet flushing. Why should toilet training be any scarier than it already is? Gentle Flush II plays dramatic classical themes to accompany toilet-based activities.

MEDICINE CABINET LOCK 'N' STOR: Medicines are simply too dangerous to keep in the home. This national chain of warehouses will rent you a small medicine cabinet far across town, five or six flights up, and double locked so that you and a Lock 'n' Stor employee must both be present with keys.

TOILET PAPER SENSOR: An alarm sounds when more than five feet of toilet paper is unrolled all at once.

THE DOLLOPATOR: This device automatically dispenses a single dollop of training toothpaste, and no more, until reset by an adult, because even these new toddler-safe training toothpastes are not, after all, a dessert topping.

For All Around the House

BICYCLE HELMETS: Not just for cycling anymore! How many bumps on the noggin will your children suffer before you realize that this light, impact-absorbing shell with Velcro chin fastener should be the first thing they put on in the morning?

CHOKE TESTER TUBE: The new and improved version no longer includes the removable lid that proved to be a hazard for children three and under.

SPRAYCOAT (PATENT PENDING): Here's a simple one-step answer to all your child-proofing needs. SprayCoat technicians cover every inch of your home with a soft, thick but transparent polymer. There'll be no hard edges anywhere, cleanups are a breeze, and you can stop feeling guilty about all the unread books on your shelves because they're permanently sealed in place.

WALL SWITCH GUARD: It's not strictly a safety item, but it will prevent kids from discovering how much "fun" it is to flick lights on and off incessantly.

INDUSTRIAL METAL LATHE SAFETY GUARDS: Don't you hate it when you have to shut down your high-speed industrial lathe, just because Junior has toddled into the workroom? Not a problem with our six-step system, which includes a child-size welder's mask, a flameproof baby jumper tested at six hundred degrees, and DON'T TOUCH THE ROTATING METAL ROD signs.

ELECTRICAL CORD CAMOUFLAGE: You've tried taping them down, buying covers, even living without electricity. Now try decorating those troublesome electrical cords with our trompe l'oeil paint kit to make them blend into wood floors, carpets, even the most intricate Oriental rugs.

Alarms

NATURAL GAS DETECTOR: Why let your home turn into a massive ticking time bomb? Will also pick up radon, carbon monoxide, methane, and even some cases of severe halitosis.

POOL ALARM: When the pool water is disturbed, it goes off. It's great for knowing when it has started raining, or when the wind is blowing.

TV RADIATION MONITOR: Measures levels that will help minimize the damage of television radiation. (Plus, we've found that when sitting forty feet from the set, kids tend to lose interest.)

GPS JR.! If you can get your kids used to wearing a global positioning tracking collar when they're little, maybe when they're teenagers they'll still go along with it.

What to Read

WARNING: SHORT DIATRIBE AHEAD!

Would you like your kid to be smart? Sure you would, and there is absolutely no mystery about how to accomplish that. The less TV they watch and the more books you read to them, the smarter they will be. There will come a time for TV, but before they can demand it, why give it to them? As soon as they will sit still in your lap, start reading them books. Read and read and read some more. In the short term, they'll learn language, learn to interpret ideas, and follow logical patterns. In the long term, they'll be smart and successful, and won't live in your basement until they are twenty-eight. See, reading *Elephant and Piggie* over and over isn't just for them; it's for your own long-term good. Okay, lecture over.

On the other hand, life is busy. The TV gives you a much-needed break. Every time you sit down to read a few good-night stories, you fall asleep before your kid does. That is a legitimate problem. Let's face it; even the best books for toddlers are pretty boring. (You don't see too many guys on the commuter train with their heads buried in *Goodnight Moon*.) There is a lot of discussion of colors and letters; cows and doggies; plenty of bold, simple colors; and not much drama. To make reading as painless as possible, try to find books that you can stand—and don't give in to your child's demand to read the same book over and over. Sure, they would enjoy it, but you've got to maintain your sanity. If you're truly dedicated, you can make trips to the library a regular part of your schedule. If not, you'll need a shelf of books that can stand up to repeated readings. There are plenty of reviews and advisers available out there; here are just a few warnings, pitfalls, and gems.

The Tale of Peter Rabbit by Beatrix Potter is a classic; a charming oh-so-British morality tale with beautiful illustrations by the author. A couple of her other books—*The Tale of Two Bad Mice* and *The Tale of Tom Kitten*—are also pleasant diversions, but do not be fooled into thinking that the twenty-three-volume complete works is a good purchase. First off, most of the stories feature main characters that are trying to eat each other. Second, the syntax is hard to parse, and the storytelling is just plain odd. And if you're confused, surely your two-year-old will be, too.

On the other hand, you can hardly go wrong with Dr. Seuss. A handful of the later books—*The Lorax* and *Oh, The Places You'll Go*—get a bit pedantic and moralistic, but everything else is a joy from cover to cover. The carefully constructed metrical rhythms put almost every other children's "poet" to shame. The more you delve into the lazy rhymes and awkward scansion in other writers, the more you'll appreciate the good Doctor.

While we're near the I Can Read It All by Myself! books in the Random House collection, do not overlook the works of P. D. Eastman, especially *Go, Dog. Go!* This book may look at first glance like exactly the wrong sort to read over and over. There are only about fifty discrete words. There is only the loosest of story lines, and every page is just more dogs, dogs at play, dogs at work, dogs going around . . . "Go around again!" And yet, through some miracle, it is, in fact, one of the most rereadable short texts ever created. Personally, I compare the prose style to early Hemingway. "The sun is up. The sun is yellow. The yellow sun is over the house." *A Farewell to Arms?* Nope. *Go, Dog. Go!*

If you're looking for something else, try Mo Willems. *Don't Let the Pigeon Drive the Bus!* and the *Knuffle Bunny* books are excellent, but the Elephant and Piggie series is the most compelling. These books are fascinating studies in minimalist comedy and illustrative timing. They're like little sitcoms in print. For four-year-olds.

When you spend enough hours poring over the great works of children's literature, you're bound to make some interesting discoveries. They say the mark of a classic is that you can always find something new in it. For example, in *Madeline* by Ludwig Bemelmans, when the lead is off in the hospital having her appendix removed, and after the eleven remaining girls have paid their visit and returned home in "two straight lines," there are still twelve little girls in the illustration "who break their bread" at dinner! A small continuity error that has been in print since 1939. It is also fun to find the little choices that authors made in earlier eras that today's editors and school librarians would no doubt squelch. When Curious George comes on board the ship in his very first adventure, the man in the yellow hat lets him smoke a pipe after dinner. That's nothing compared with the cannibals that attack Babar and Celeste on their honeymoon. Just more good reasons to read—all the odd things you'll find yourself explaining to a three-year-old.

What to Expect in Your Cart

Not all that long ago, there was an exciting phenomenon called the postpartum postal deluge. As soon as America's legal conspiracy—mail-order marketing lists—registers that you have been blessed with a bouncing baby consumer, the catalogs began pouring into your home. Today, the American marketing machine comes into your home much more cost effectively through the Internet.

Unsolicited e-mails, mom-group buying discounts, purchased search results, cookies. They will find you. And they know you will buy. And you know it, too. We as a nation are always willing to spend whatever money we have on our kids. Recession or depression, our instinct to provide, coddle, and delight takes over. Even as we drive that nine-year-old Toyota into the ground, clip coupons, tuck Tupperware into the briefcase, and take vacations in the backyard, we are still willing to recite our magic number (and expiration date) to an operator so that the kids can each have "a wooden puzzle of their own first name."

Or an adorable lavender-and-mint jumpsuit from Hanna Andersson. Or a couple of pairs of those Sara's Prints pajamas—the ones that aren't actually called pajamas because the government won't allow plain cotton items to be sold as sleepwear because it's not fire retardant, but you know and we know that they *are* pajamas. Ooh, more links. While we're getting 100 percent cotton, let's click up a couple of those organic cotton "onesies" for infants from The Natural Baby and a few sweatshirts from Gymboree (formerly a gym/birthday party center—now a national clothing chain), or maybe the sweatshirts in After the Stork are better, or cheaper? We'll take both. Say, how did I get on the Disney site? Oh, well, hit me with a couple of videos, and the Donald Duck slippers. Don't babies need slippers? Add to shopping cart! Back to Basics?—classic toys—we'll take whatever we used to have when we were kids—fun or not.

Are we spoiling this baby? Let's see what we can get that'll really be good for them. Aha, we'll take the metric number rods from Early Learning Center, the marble run from Sensational Beginnings, the big block set, oh, free shipping? Well, make it the really big one. Something from Right Start—whatever, it just sounds like a good place to order—send us two of your finest dress-up outfits and throw in some face paints. HearthSong? Some finger paints or finger puppets or both—do you have any paint-puppets? That should do it for now. Oh, wait! Oriental Trading Company! The official home of party-favor toys and themed junk, and the best place to buy when you're buying a "gross" of anything.

And eBay! I'm searching for Rock 'Em Sock 'Em Robots . . . not that new one, the actual version I had in 1985—omigosh, a complete vintage set of Wacky Packages stickers! Just what Baby needs!

Going Back to Work

"Can I go back to work yet?"

Ah, yes, work. The halcyon place where coffee breaks are not broken dreams—they actually happen. A place where screaming, wailing, sobbing, and moaning are reserved for those infrequent discussions of salary. Most important of all, it's a place where each individual is responsible for his or her own bathroom needs. It's a place full of grown-ups, relative peace, and relative quiet.

And no, you can't go back to work. You've got time off, mister. You've come a long way, Baby. Paternity leave is more and more common, thanks to more flexible work schedules, more progressive corporate attitudes, and management's realization that a man who isn't sleeping through the night is a liability anyway. When it all seems to be too much, remember that before long—a few weeks, at most a few months—you'll be back in the rat race, the lovely, predictable, satisfying nine-to-five. Your wife can take care of the home front. Or best of all, you can both go back to work and hire someone to raise your children. Remember, never *ever* say, even jokingly, that you'd love to stay home and be the primary caretaker. Sure, it'll make you sound hip, but you may later have the words *verbal contract* flung in your face.

Safety Can Be Fun

"We've childproofed every last corner of our home, but when I look at some of the toys we've got, frankly, I get scared. How can we know what's safe?"

After childproofing your home, it would be foolish to outfit your child with toys that are death traps—things like balloons (choking hazard) and wooden blocks (sharp edges, weight); so be sure to use common sense in choosing playthings. It's not easy to find toys that are truly, thoroughly safe, but here are some basic items that we especially recommend for the safety-conscious parent:

NO-GO BIKE: It looks just like the real thing, but your kids can push the pedals all day long without risky movement.

SPONGE BLOCKS: Old-fashioned wooden blocks are too hard, and these stack almost as well and double as cleaning accessories for those major spills.

TEDDY BORE: What's the danger in traditional stuffed animals? Kids can get too attached to their favorite, dragging it everywhere and drooling on it, among other things, and this can create a sanitary disaster area of a toy. The Teddy Bore is specially designed and thoroughly tested; he will not have any lasting appeal to most children. His humorless expression, scratchy surface, and faint mildewy odor guarantee it.

CRAYON-ISH NONMARKERS: Sixty-four fabulous colors, neatly sorted and labeled, able to be dumped out, sorted, broken, peeled, tasted, and dumped out again—but completely unable to make a mark! That's right, these inert plastic cylinders won't mark walls, floors, or activity books!

Let's Do It Again

Q. *"The baby is sure cute and fun, but that wasn't easy. Still, I guess at some point we'll be back."*

A. No baby's life is complete without a sibling! Yes, you are going to do it all again. The biggest question is timing. A neat two years is the industry standard, but some wait longer, others accidentally do it sooner. The advantage of two years is that three- and four-year-olds are much more likely to be pissed off when they confront "sharing" for the first time. A two-year-old doesn't know any better. As for bigger lags, just remember that once you haven't seen a diaper or three a.m. in a while, it can feel like a real setback to be there again.

No matter how long it has been since your first baby, the main difference in a second pregnancy is that the mystery is over. Even if the second time is quite different in its particulars, you at least have something to compare it with. This will give you a useful baseline of information, but don't get too blasé. Sure, you won't bother to take the birth-readiness class, but it is worth giving yourself a refresher course on the stages of labor, what to do in an emergency, and so forth. Finally, your biggest challenge may be figuring out who can take over caring for the new big sister/brother suddenly in the middle of the night. Bringing them along is not an option. And home birth is a fairly extreme solution to a little logistical snag.

Anything beyond the second time is irrelevant from a pregnancy guidebook point of view because no one who is expecting a third child sits down and reads a pregnancy guidebook, even a very funny one. They don't have time, for one thing. For another, they figure they've been there, done that.

Nonetheless, it is worth considering your future. As a fertile friend once pointed out, when you wave in the third child, you and your wife have to shift from man-to-man defense to a zone, and nothing will ever be the same. Expectations shift from nurturing and educating to simple survival and meeting state-mandated parenting requirements. Also, you can probably get away with the "three is the new two" argument, but when you go to four or more, you're just showing off, and we all know it.

Flying Babies

We really want to take our baby to my parents for Christmas, but that means a long airplane flight. When will the baby be ready to fly? And what can we do to prepare?"

The one great thing about flying with an infant is that, for once, your appearance with Baby in your arms will *not* be greeted with oohs and aahs of admiration. As you walk down the aisle, all eyes will be upon you, but the looks will communicate thinly veiled dread that your seat will be near. It's a pleasant change.

Actually, traveling with an infant is much easier than traveling with babies a year or older. The bell curve of misery peaks at about two-and-a-half. But it remains fairly miserable up to age twelve, when traveling becomes easy again because your child will simply remain sullen and quiet, hoping to achieve the effect that they are, in fact, traveling alone. Up until that age, anything can happen. An infant may be lulled to sleep by the plane's vibration and the white noise of the engines. Or the baby will scream holy murder from start to finish.

If babies had been meant to fly they would have been born with more fully developed inner ear systems. As it is, uncomfortable air pressure during descent and ascent affects them more

than it does adults. Prepare a bottle and have it ready, as swallowing can alleviate the discomfort. Another handy tip: Teach your two-month-old infant how to chew gum, which will ease the air pressure, help with teething, and give a charming "wizened street urchin" look.

The Farmer in the Dell

"Call me selfish, but I think I'll lose my mind if I have to drive around listening to vapid children's music compilations of 'Head, Shoulders, Knees, and Toes' or 'Whistle While You Work.'"

Have no fear! While there are still frightening CD collections of Barney, Raffi, Disney, and those generic "various" artists all singing the same grating kids' songs ("Here We Go Loopty Loo," "Frère Jacques," and "This Old Man" in particular have the ability to freeze the soul), more and more legitimately cool artists have seen the need for kids' music that parents can stand. Look for They Might Be Giants, Tom Chapin, Dan Zanes, and Buckwheat Zydeco.

Of course, the problem is that little kids don't particularly like these albums. When they get old enough to compromise, try classic Sesame Street albums and the Backyardigans. Or just play The Beatles and think of it as an important part of their education.

Superman Syndrome

Q. *"We've heard all about the modern-day 'superwoman' juggling career and motherhood, but what about us? Am I wrong in feeling that I've fallen into a Superman syndrome—trying to do it all?"*

A. We may be going out on a limb, but it's fair to say that trying to balance family and career can be just as difficult for a man as for a woman. Maybe *more* difficult. Yeah, more difficult, that's it. The pressures and expectations are just too much—we have no role models. Our own fathers were absent or misinformed or probably both. Today's father drives himself crazy trying to be the perfect supportive and dedicated husband, the merciless career juggernaut at work, and still a loyal pal to the boys in the poker circle.

It's up at four A.M. on Saturdays to go trout fishing (an important commune with nature), then back to the house by nine to make waffles, then you've got to get the groceries and do the laundry in time to sit back and enjoy the afternoon's ball game. While jogging in place (you did sit-ups and push-ups earlier) so you don't go completely to pot, whip up a stew for dinner, do the dishes, repair that kitchen drawer that keeps falling out, repaint the bathroom, and then run out and pick up the dry cleaning. It's one thing after another, and, all together, too exhausting.

When the baby comes, you will simply have to make choices. No man can be a scratch golfer and bake from scratch, too. And golfing is more fun than baking. So relax. You'll just have to settle for second best now and then. You can't "do it all," so don't try. Be ready to compromise once in a while. If you need to stay late at the office, stay; she'll understand. If you need to take the boys from the office out to a great new batting cage, she'll understand. But cut a few corners at work, too. Try making a short phone call to your wife from work, just to see how she's doing—the few minutes you lose won't cost you that promotion—and it would mean a lot to her. There are plenty of ways to show her you care. You could cash in your chips and leave the poker game in time to get home for the two A.M. feeding, just for one example.

Little things like that mean a lot to a new mother. And if all the pressures just seem to be too much, hit the panic button and escape. Think: When was the last time you did something just for you? Take a weekend "off" from the home front and play thirty-six holes of golf. The more relaxed and happy you are, the better a helpmate you'll be when you *are* around. Right?

Oh, well, they seemed like good ideas to us.

Postpartum Medical School Syndrome

Q. *"My wife just had a baby, and now she has decided she wants to go to medical school and become a doctor. She seems quite serious about this. Will it wear off?"*

A. It may seem strange, but the PMS[2] trend is becoming more and more common. Postpartum medical school syndrome occurs in varying degrees in one out of four new mothers. For some, it is only a bothersome regret that they didn't pay more attention in tenth-grade biology. For others, it leads to years of training and an MD.

Why does it happen? Well, a little knowledge is a dangerous thing. Your wife has done nine months of intensive reading in pregnancy books, which present detailed medical information and are also full of criticism of the male hegemony in the medical profession, which is blamed for everything from the high rate of cesareans to the parking problems around the hospital.

After all this research into medical possibilities, options in anesthesia, hospital regulations, and obstetrical innovations, your wife—no matter what her career up to this point—will feel that she missed her true calling and that she must become a doctor. So you are not alone, and it is certainly foolish to oppose your wife's wishes. Why try to stop her when the complexities of first-year biochemistry will probably do the job, without all the emotional underpinnings, the failure to be supportive, and all that?

And if she does become a doctor, look on the bright side: Now you can play golf together.

Success

Q. *"I don't want to push my kid, but I do want to make sure that he's stimulated and enriched and . . . all right, I do want to push my kid, okay?"*

A. Everybody wants their baby to grow up happy and generous, socially graceful and successful, well educated, with a profession, impressive titles, advanced degrees, loads of money, world travel, a wonderful spouse, perfect grandchildren. You want for them all the things you can brag about. Everybody wants these things, but only the people who want them most will get them. The future is now. What will you teach your baby today? Who will they be tomorrow?

Looking out for number one is more than just good changing table advice. From day one, you've got to instill a winning attitude in your infant. After all, nice babies finish last. So push your kids! Teach them how to maneuver office politics, dress them for success, make them remember the full name of everyone they meet (to better win friends and influence people). Instruct them on how to manipulate social situations to get what they want, how to avoid dorky kids, and how to properly fold a business letter. Let them eat the olives from your martinis, give them every possible privilege, and, of course, teach them not to take no for an answer. You'll get just the kids you deserve.

What Did You Expect?

Now you're on your own. You've read *What to Expect When Your Wife Is Expanding*, you've studied the advice and information, you've even looked up the hard words. You have devoted time and energy to preparing yourself for the dawn of fatherhood. Well done. Without intelligent, devoted readers like you, a moneymaking sequel, fact-each-day calendar, sale of the film rights, or fourth edition would be impossible.

We have made every effort to be absolutely complete in our coverage of the issues and possibilities of pregnancy. We feel certain that answers to all your questions lie in these pages. Although we just realized that we forgot to write up that piece on taking a nonstress test—don't worry, there's nothing to it, really. Oh, shoot, we didn't say anything about the pros and cons of flu shots or choosing a godparent, either. I suppose it's a little late now. And we fully intended to provide a thorough

discussion of the pros and cons of cesarean births from the father's perspective, but you can figure it out for yourselves. We did mention Montgomery's tubercles, didn't we? Pretty sure we did. And bonding? We didn't do bonding, either? Well, it's important, so do it, and that's all you really need to know. Listen, maybe it wouldn't be such a bad idea to get a hold of some *other* guidebook to pregnancy, just sort of as a way to double-check. Oh, shoot, we definitely should have done that feature on emergency delivery when you don't get to the hospital on time.

Dads-to-be, just remember this: You can be pregnant and funny, but a hysterical pregnancy is no pregnancy at all. We're not sure what that means. But if you just remember it, maybe it'll keep you from worrying about other things too much.

Have a great pregnancy, a wonderful outcome—oh, and give our best regards to your wife.

Recommended Reading

Acredolo, Linda, and Susan Goodwyn. *Baby Signs: How to Talk With Your Baby Before Your Baby Can Talk*, 3rd ed. New York: McGraw-Hill, 2009.

Arms, Suzanne. *Immaculate Deception*. Boston: Houghton-Mifflin, 1975.

Brazelton, T. Berry. *Infants & Mothers*. New York: Delacorte, 1969.

Cannon, Hall, ed. *Cowboy Poetry: A Gathering*. Layton, UT: Gibbs M. Smith, 1985.

Cerf, Bennett. *Riddle-De-Dee*. New York: Ballantine, 1962.

Dick-Read, Grantley. *Childbirth Without Fear*. New York: Harper & Row, 1972.

Eiger, Marvin S., and Sally Wendkos Olds. *The Complete Book of Breastfeeding*. New York: Bantam, 1973.

Hill, Thomas. *TV Land To Go: The Big Book of TV Lists, TV Lore, and TV Bests*. New York: Simon & Schuster/Fireside, 2001.

Hill, Thomas. *What the Heck Were You Expecting? A Complete Guide for the Perplexed Father*. New York: Three Rivers Press, 2000.

Kunhardt, Dorothy. *Pat the Bunny*. New York: Western Publishing, 1991.

Leach, Penelope. *Your Baby & Child*. New York: Knopf, 1978.

Leboyer, Frederick. *Birth Without Violence*. New York: Knopf, 1975.

Lewis, Michael. *Moneyball: The Art of Winning an Unfair Game*. New York: W. W. Norton, 2003.

Mayo Clinic. *Mayo Clinic Guide to a Healthy Pregnancy*. Intercourse, PA: Good Books, 2011.

Murkoff, Heidi, and Sharon Mazel. *What to Expect When You're Expecting, 4th ed.* New York: Workman Publishing, 2008.

Murkoff, Heidi. *What to Expect: Eating Well When You're Expecting.* New York: Workman Publishing, 2005.

Murkoff, Heidi. *What to Expect Before You're Expecting.* New York: Workman Publishing, 2009.

Perec, Georges, and Gilbert Adair, trans. *A Void.* London: Harvill/Harper Collins, 1995.

Schmidt, Philip. *Black & Decker The Complete Guide: Build Your Kids a Treehouse.* Chanhassen, MN: Creative Publishing International, 2007.

Steig, Irwin. *Poker for Fun and Profit.* New York: Astor-Honor, 1959.

Walker, Brian, ed. *The Best of Ernie Bushmiller's Nancy.* New York: Henry Holt, 1988.

Weddle, Ethel H. *Walter Chrysler: Boy Machinist.* Childhood of Famous American Series. New York: Bobbs-Merrill, 1960.